Disciplinary and Grievance Procedures

Employment Law Supplement

June 2009

Incomes Data Services Ltd
Finsbury Tower, 103-105 Bunhill Row, London, EC1Y 8LZ
Tel: 020 7429 6800 Fax: 020 7393 8081

Website: www.incomesdata.co.uk

ISBN 978-1-847-03968-2

IDS Employment Law Supplement, 'Disciplinary and Grievance Procedures', is published by Incomes Data Services Limited (Registered in England & Wales, Company No 913794. Registered Office and address for service: 100 Avenue Road, London NW3 3PF).

This publication aims to provide accurate, authoritative information and comment on the subjects it covers. It is offered to subscribers on the understanding that the publisher is not in business as a lawyer or consultant.

No natural forests were destroyed to make this product: only farmed timber was used and re-planted.

A CIP catalogue record for this book is available from the British Library.

Printed by St Austell Printing Co, 41 Truro Road, St Austell, Cornwall PL25 5JE

Contents

Introduction

On 6 April 2009, the statutory dispute resolution procedures (SDRPs) that were introduced just four and a half years previously by the Employment Act 2002 were repealed. It is unlikely that many mourned their passing, since the procedures were much maligned by employment judges, lawyers and tribunal users alike for their over-complicated, prescriptive provisions and the draconian consequences that accompanied a failure to comply with them. These included employees being denied the right to a hearing of their claim and employers facing findings of automatically unfair dismissal for procedural failings.

The SDRPs failed to achieve the Government's desired effect of reducing the number of claims issued in employment tribunals by encouraging parties to resolve issues within the workplace first. Instead, the Government-commissioned review carried out by Michael Gibbons ('the Gibbons Review') concluded that the statutory procedures, while well intentioned, were 'inappropriately inflexible and prescriptive' and had had the unintended consequence of formalising action at an earlier stage. They had also spawned a huge amount of satellite litigation concerning their interpretation. The Gibbons Review recommended the repeal of the entire SDRP regime and its replacement with 'clear, simple, non-prescriptive guidelines on grievances, discipline and dismissal'. A period of public consultation followed, culminating in the repeal of the SDRPs by the Employment Act 2008 and the introduction of a revised Acas Code of Practice on Disciplinary and Grievances Procedures and a new S.207A of the Trade Union and Labour Relations (Consolidation) Act 1992 (TULR(C)A). This provision gives employment tribunals the discretion to increase or decrease the amount of compensation awarded in a relevant claim by up to 25 per cent if the employer or employee has 'unreasonably' failed to comply with the Code.

The new regime is considerably more flexible than the old one and allows for a common-sense approach that was absent from the SDRPs. However, it is not entirely trouble free and it is unlikely that we have seen the end of legal arguments in this area. For example, there is some confusion over what constitutes a 'grievance' under the Acas Code and there is also lack of clarity over the application of the Code in cases of long-term incapacity on grounds of ill health and other 'no fault' dismissals. Furthermore, the Code specifically excludes dismissals on grounds of redundancy and the non-renewal of fixed-term contracts on their expiry (even though case authorities have established that procedural fairness is still an essential test of reasonableness in such cases), which could prove costly if the wrong label is used And finally, submissions about whether a failure to follow the Code was or was not 'unreasonable' are likely to be common in remedies hearings as the parties argue over whether an adjustment to the award should be made.

While the SDRPs were certainly counterproductive in terms of achieving their stated goal of reducing traffic through the employment tribunals system, they

i

did at least introduce minimum standards of dispute resolution into the workplace and the prospect of a financial penalty for failing to comply with the Acas Code is an incentive to maintain those standards. Whether the prospect of a financial penalty will reduce pressure on the tribunal system is another matter. With significant adjustments to the amount of compensation awarded at stake, the temptation to involve lawyers in a dispute will be high. Nor are the short time limits for bringing an employment tribunal claim conducive to early dispute resolution: in most cases, a tribunal claim must be presented within three months of the act complained of (e.g. dismissal) and the three-month extension to the time limit that applied under the SDRPs has been abandoned. While the Code and the accompanying non-statutory Acas Guide, 'Discipline and grievances at work', encourage parties to try mediation to resolve disputes, there is no compulsion to do so and the goal of alternative dispute resolution in place of litigation remains a long way off.

In this Supplement we explain the provisions of the new Acas Code of Practice and discuss the appropriate procedures for dealing with disciplinary action, dismissals and grievances under the new regime in accordance with the Code, where it applies; the relevant legislation; and case authorities. For details of the old law under the SDRPs, see the IDS Supplement, 'Statutory Disciplinary and Grievance Procedures' (2004).

Scheme of the Supplement

The scheme of this Supplement is as follows:

- Chapter 1 sets out the new legal framework and details the provisions of the revised Acas Code of Practice. It also outlines changes to the Acas pre-claim conciliation service and explains the transitional provisions that determine which regime applies

- Chapter 2 gives guidance on the drafting and implementation of a discipline and grievance policy

- Chapter 3 describes the procedures that should be followed in relation to the various types of disciplinary action and dismissal, both where the Acas Code applies and where it does not

- Chapter 4 explains the common law duty on employers to deal with its employees' grievances and considers the definition of a grievance. It goes on to look at the procedural steps required by the Acas Code

- Chapter 5 focuses on the consequences for employers and employees who fail to follow fair procedures, considering liability in relation to dismissals and in respect of the discriminatory handling of procedures. It also looks at the compensation adjustment provisions contained in new S.207A TULR(C)A

- Chapter 6 explains the statutory right to be accompanied at disciplinary and grievance hearings

- Chapter 7 provides an overview of alternative dispute resolution methods, such as mediation, and considers whether the post-SDRP regime effects a change in the culture of dispute resolution generally.

The law is stated as at 15 May 2009.

> **This publication aims to provide accurate, authoritative information and comment on the subjects it covers. It is offered to subscribers on the understanding that the publisher is not in business as a lawyer or consultant.**

1 The legal framework

The Acas Code of Practice

Adjustment to tribunal awards

Consequential amendments

Transitional provisions

For a four-and-a-half year period from October 2004 to April 2009, disciplinary and grievance procedures at work were governed by the Employment Act 2002 and the Employment Act 2002 (Dispute Resolution) Regulations 2004 SI 2004/752. These required all employers to have written disciplinary and grievance procedures that incorporated at least the minimum elements of a fair procedure as set out in the statutory dismissal and disciplinary procedures (DDPs) and the statutory grievance procedures (GPs), together known as the statutory dispute resolution procedures (SDRPs). Those procedures, which are explained fully in IDS Employment Law Supplement, 'Statutory Disciplinary and Grievance Procedures' (2004), consisted of a standard three-step procedure for use in most cases and a modified two-step procedure that could be used in certain circumstances when the employment contract had come to an end.

However, the SDRPs failed to achieve the Government's desired effect of reducing the number of claims issued in employment tribunals in favour of resolution within the workplace. Instead, the overly prescriptive and complicated legislation in many cases accelerated the litigation process, with both parties seeking legal advice at an earlier stage to ensure compliance. Rather than promoting informal resolution, it therefore encouraged parties to put things in writing and formalised disputes at an early stage. The procedures also spawned a huge amount of satellite litigation on how they should be applied and were widely criticised by employment tribunal users, judges and legal advisers. A failure to comply could lead to draconian consequences, with employees being denied the right to a hearing of their claim and employers facing findings of automatically unfair dismissal for procedural failings.

In response to the criticisms levelled at the new procedures, in December 2006 the Government commissioned Michael Gibbons, a member of the Better Regulation Commission, to carry out a review of the dispute resolution and employment tribunal process ('the Gibbons Review'). His conclusions, 'Better Dispute Resolution: A review of employment dispute resolution in Great Britain', published by the Department of Trade and Industry (now the Department for Business, Enterprise and Regulatory Reform) in March 2007, were that, while well-intentioned, the SDRPs had 'failed to produce the desired

1

policy outcome' and provided a classic example of 'good policy, but inappropriately inflexible and prescriptive regulation'. He recommended the complete repeal of the 2004 statutory procedures and their replacement with a system that was less prescriptive but still allowed employment tribunals to take the use of fair procedures into account when assessing compensation.

The Government responded to the Gibbons review with a period of public consultation that culminated in the introduction of new dispute resolution provisions contained in the Employment Act 2008 (EA 08). This repealed Ss.29–33 of and Schedules 2 to 4 to the Employment Act 2002, the Employment Act 2002 (Dispute Resolution) Regulations 2004 SI 2004/752, and S.98A of the Employment Rights Act 1996 – the provision that makes a dismissal automatically unfair if the employer has failed to follow a relevant DDP – as from 6 April 2009, and instead made provision for employment tribunals to adjust compensatory awards upwards or downwards according to adherence to a revised Acas Code of Practice on discipline and grievance. Consequently, on that date the statutory DDPs and GPs ceased to apply to new disputes and it is no longer essential to follow a three-step disciplinary and dismissal or grievance procedure. Instead, parties are expected to comply with the revised Acas Code of Practice on Discipline and Grievance Procedures, a failure to follow which can result in an adjustment in compensation of up to 25 per cent in a subsequent employment tribunal claim. However, it should be noted that the SDRPs did not disappear overnight and continue to apply to disputes that *arose* before 6 April but are awaiting a tribunal hearing, as well as to those that *started* before 6 April but continued after that date; for example, cases of ongoing discrimination or constructive dismissal based on cumulative events – see 'Transitional provisions' below.

This chapter explains the principles behind the revised Acas Code, the circumstances in which it applies and the provisions relating to the adjustment of awards. It also details consequential changes made following the repeal of the statutory procedures and explains the transitional provisions that determine when the outgoing procedures continue to apply.

The Acas Code of Practice

The revised Code of Practice on Disciplinary and Grievance Procedures ('the Code') was issued under S.199 of the Trade Union and Labour Relations (Consolidation) Act 1992 (TULR(C)A), which gives Acas the power to issue Codes of Practice containing 'practical guidance… for the purpose of promoting the improvement of industrial relations'. It came into effect on 6 April 2009, replacing the Code issued in 2004 ('the 2004 Code'), and is available on the Acas website (www.acas.org.uk/drr). In accordance with S.207

TULR(C)A, the revised Code is admissible in any employment tribunal proceedings and the tribunal is obliged to take into account any relevant provision of the Code when determining those proceedings. A breach of the Code does not in itself give rise to legal proceedings but a failure by either party to abide by its provisions will be taken into account by a tribunal as evidence when determining a relevant claim.

In addition, if the claim falls under one of the relevant jurisdictions, the tribunal can increase an award of compensation by up to 25 per cent if it finds that the employer has unreasonably failed to follow the Code, or decrease it by up to 25 per cent if the employee has unreasonably failed to follow it, if it considers it just and equitable in all the circumstances to do so – new S.207A TULR(C)A (inserted by the EA 08). The tribunal jurisdictions to which the compensation adjustments apply are set out in a new Schedule A2 to the TULR(C)A (also inserted by the EA 08) and are listed in Appendix 1 to this Supplement. They cover most tribunal claims, but notable exceptions include claims under the Part-time Workers (Prevention of Less Favourable Treatment) Regulations 2000 SI 2000/1551, the Fixed-term Employees (Prevention of Less Favourable Treatment) Regulations 2002 SI 2002/2034, and the Transfer of Employees (Protection of Employment) Regulations 2006 SI 2006/246. Rights to time off work under Part VI ERA and to request flexible working under Part VIIIA are also omitted from Schedule A2.

The Code is only 11 pages long and consists of four sections: a Foreword, an Introduction, a section on handling disciplinary issues and a section on handling grievances. The Foreword does not form part of the statutory Code itself and tribunals are not required to take it into account when determining a case. It explains that the Code sets out the 'basic requirements of fairness' and is 'intended to provide the standard of reasonable behaviour in most instances'. The Foreword contains a number of general aspirations; for example, that employers and employees should always seek to resolve disciplinary and grievance issues in the workplace and that where this is not possible, they should consider using an independent third party as a mediator. It also advises employers to keep a written record of any disciplinary and grievance cases they deal with and suggests that organisations may wish to consider dealing with issues involving bullying, harassment or whistleblowing under a separate procedure.

Accompanying the Code is an 82-page non-statutory guide, 'Discipline and grievances at work ('the Acas guide'), that provides more detailed advice and guidance, much of which was taken from the 2004 Code. It is designed to complement the Code and contains a number of sample disciplinary and grievance procedures. However, tribunals are not obliged to take this Guide into account when reaching a decision. The Guide is also available on the Acas website (www.acas.org.uk/drr).

3

When does the Code apply?

As mentioned above, the Code is admissible in evidence in *any* tribunal proceedings and any provision of the Code that is relevant to any question arising must be taken into account in determining that question – S.207 TULR(C)A. In other words, any *relevant* provision of the Code must be taken into account by the tribunal when considering the issue of liability. But since the Code is designed 'to help employers, employees and their representatives deal with disciplinary and grievance situations in the workplace', it is really only relevant – for the purpose of determining *liability* – in unfair dismissal claims, or at least those involving misconduct or poor performance (note that redundancy dismissals and the non-renewal of fixed-term contracts are specifically excluded from the ambit of the Code – see below). A breach of the provisions, which are designed to ensure the application of fair procedures, could not, for example, establish liability in complaints involving sex discrimination or equal pay.

When it comes to the adjustment of compensation awards under S.207A TULR(C)A, however, the Code has much wider application since it applies to *all* claims under the jurisdictions listed in Schedule A2 to the TULR(C)A (see Appendix 1) – in so far as they relate to disciplinary or grievance situations. It is unclear how this will work in practice but there is potential, for example, for an unlawful deduction of wages claim to attract an uplift if the employer has failed to allow the employee to appeal, or for compensation to be reduced in a discrimination claim if the employee has failed to raise a grievance or attend a grievance meeting.

The Code's application to different disciplinary situations is considered in Chapter 3. Its application to grievances, which are defined as 'concerns, problems or complaints that employees raise with their employers', is discussed in Chapter 4.

Redundancy and fixed-term contracts. As mentioned above, the Code states that it does not apply to dismissals due to redundancy or the non-renewal of fixed-term contracts on their expiry – see para 1. There is a danger here that if the Code isn't followed because the employer believes, for example, that there is a redundancy situation, he may be exposed to the uplift where a tribunal finds that the employee was dismissed for a reason covered by the Code, such as sex discrimination. Also, somewhat confusingly, the adjustment can be applied to complaints involving redundancy payments, although not to complaints about redundancy dismissals. Redundancy dismissals and the expiry of fixed-term contracts are discussed further in Chapter 3.

Collective grievances. The final paragraph of the Code makes it clear that it does not apply to grievances raised on behalf of two or more employees by a trade union or workplace representative. Such grievances should be handled in accordance with the organisation's collective grievance process – para 45.

Employees only. Like the now repealed SDRPs, the Code applies only to 'employees' – i.e. those who work under a contract of employment. Although the Code does not say so, it presumably has in mind S.230 ERA, which states that a contract of employment is a 'contract of service or apprenticeship, whether express or implied, and (if it is express) whether oral or in writing'. This means that the procedures in the Code do not apply in relation to individuals who are self-employed or are categorised as 'workers' rather than employees; for example, certain types of contract worker and agency worker (the right to claim unfair dismissal is, in any event, only available to employees and not workers). New S.207A TULR(C)A (which gives tribunals the power to adjust compensation for a breach of the Code) also applies only to 'employees', as defined by S.295 TULR(C)A, which has the same restrictive definition as in the ERA. This is so despite the fact that several of the jurisdictions listed in Schedule A2 to the TULR(C)A (to which the adjustment of awards provisions in S.207A apply) appertain to both workers and employees.

This distinction is likely to cause some confusion and it may therefore be sensible for all disciplinary and grievance situations to be dealt with under the same procedure, especially given that some tribunals are likely to apply the good practice principles promoted by the Code to cases involving workers in any event. Furthermore, a person's employment status is not always obvious. As with the statutory procedures, where an employer is unsure about the employment status of a worker, he would be well advised to comply with the provisions of the Code. If he does not, and a tribunal subsequently finds the individual to have been an employee, the employer might find a tribunal taking the Code's provisions into account, as well as applying the uplift to compensation. Similar issues may arise where individuals who do not realise that they are employees fail to comply with the Code.

One slight anomaly of the Code is that it includes the recommendation that the employer allow an employee to be accompanied to a disciplinary or grievance hearing (paras 13–16 and 34–37). The right to be accompanied, which is discussed in Chapter 6, is a statutory right under S.10 of the Employment Relations Act 1999 (ERelA) that applies to both workers and employees. This is therefore one 'recommendation' that cannot be ignored and excused on the ground of reasonableness and it is important that employers allow both workers and employees to be accompanied (another reason why employers may choose to have the same procedures for both). An employer's failure to allow a worker to be accompanied under S.10 entitles the worker to claim compensation of up to two weeks' pay (subject to the statutory cap on a week's pay, currently £350) in accordance with S.11 ERelA. The consequence of this right appearing in the Code is that *employees* who have been refused the right to be accompanied could be awarded an uplift in compensation under S.207A TULR(C)A in addition to any remedy claimed under the ERelA. In practice, of course, tribunals are free to decide that if an employee has already made a complaint under S.11 it would not be just and equitable to increase his or her compensation under S.207A. However, as with all aspects of the Code, it will be for individual tribunals to consider what is just and equitable in the particular circumstances.

Former employees. It is unclear whether the Code applies to grievances raised by former employees once the employment relationship has ended. Under the old statutory regime, former employers and employees could agree to use the special modified grievance procedure in these circumstances. However, there is no equivalent procedure in the new Code and no mention of whether the Code applies in respect of post-employment grievances. Until there is clarification on this point from the courts, we would advise both employers and employees to assume that the Code does apply post-termination to avoid a potential adjustment being made to an award for failure to follow the Code. This approach is bolstered by the fact that S.207A TULR(C)A, which governs the adjustment of awards where there has been an unreasonable failure to comply with the Code, applies to breach of contract claims under the Employment Tribunal Extension of Jurisdiction (England and Wales) Order 1994 SI 1994/1624 (see Schedule A2 TULR(C)A – set out in Appendix 1 to this Supplement). A claim under the 1994 Order can *only* be presented to a tribunal where it arises or is outstanding on the termination of employment, implying that the Code applies in these circumstances.

Employees with less than one year's service. The right to claim 'ordinary' unfair dismissal under S.98 ERA is only available to employees with more than one year's service. However, employers should not simply assume that they can ignore the Code in respect of employees with less than a year's service, as many of the jurisdictions covered by S.207A TULR(C)A are not dependent on any minimum period of employment and there is no guarantee that such claims will not be brought. For example, wrongful dismissal claims – where the dismissal is in breach of contract as no or insufficient notice (or pay in lieu) has been given – are covered by S.207A, with the result that the uplift may be applied to an award of damages regardless of whether the employee has sufficient service to bring an unfair dismissal claim.

Constructive dismissal. The Code is unclear on whether it is intended to apply in constructive dismissal cases, and if so, how. Under the SDRPs, the statutory GPs applied, meaning that a constructively dismissed employee was obliged to raise a grievance before bringing a tribunal claim. While a failure to raise a grievance in accordance with the new Code will not bar a claim, it is possible that any compensation awarded will be reduced under S.207A to reflect non-compliance.

Failure to comply by one party. The Code is silent as to whether one party is still bound to follow the Code when the other party has failed to comply. This is likely to come down to the type and extent of failure involved and whether it

6

was reasonable for the party not in breach to treat him or herself as released from any further obligations under the Code. A minor breach is unlikely to render the whole Code unworkable, particularly given the fairly non-prescriptive language used, and it may therefore be unreasonable to treat it as bringing all obligations to an end.

General principles

Despite what many commentators have said, the abolition of the SDRPs has not simply meant a return to the pre-2004 regime. Although that regime involved an earlier version of the Acas Code of Practice, which tribunals were obliged to take into account under S.207 TULR(C)A in the same way as they must now take the revised Code into account, not only is the content of the new Code different, but it allows tribunals to impose financial penalties for non-compliance in a way that the old one did not. This added financial incentive will no doubt focus parties' minds on the new Code in a way they were not focused before. And it is not just employers who face financial penalties for failing to comply – employees risk having their compensation reduced for, for example, failing to attend a disciplinary meeting or failing to appeal, with the result that employees are now far more likely to pay heed to the Code than was previously the case.

There is clearly a nudge towards mediation in the revised Code, reflecting the recommendations of the Gibbons review. However, there is no compulsion to try mediation since the statement that 'employers and employees should always seek to resolve disciplinary and grievance issues in the workplace' and, where this is not possible, to 'consider using an independent third party to help resolve the problem' is contained in the Foreword, which does not form part of the statutory Code itself, and a failure to do so will therefore not be a breach of the Code. Despite Gibbons' recommendations and the Government's intention to promote mediation as an alternative to litigation, some commentators believe that the formalisation of disciplinary and grievance procedures that came about as an unintended consequence of the introduction of the statutory procedures has effected a change in culture that is now irreversible. There are, however, some changes to the services offered by Acas as a result of the Gibbons' review recommendations, including a new pre-claim conciliation service, which are explained later in this chapter under 'Consequential amendments'.

The Code takes into account the size and resources of the employer, allowing employers flexibility to depart from aspects of the Code in certain circumstances if it is reasonable to do so – see para 3. This is not a new concept in unfair dismissal law since the size and administrative resources of the employer are already a factor in the test of reasonableness under S.98(4) ERA. However, there is a risk in departing from the Code since employers will be banking on an employment tribunal agreeing that their departure was reasonable. As anyone with experience of unfair dismissal cases knows, one

7

employer's – and one tribunal's – perception of reasonableness is not always the same as another's.

The new scheme has a number of advantages. Gone are the complicated exceptions and deemed compliance provisions of the statutory procedures and employees are no longer barred from bringing claims for failing to issue a grievance. There is no automatic penalty for a failure to follow any of the steps – instead, tribunals must take into account all the circumstances and can only impose a financial penalty if they consider that such a failure was 'unreasonable' and that it is just and equitable to do so. This gives employers and tribunals a flexibility in their approach that was lacking under the previous regime, as it allows for circumstances in which it would be reasonable to disregard some of the Acas recommendations.

However, there is less certainty in the current approach since what an employer considers to be reasonable may not be seen in the same light by a tribunal, and there may be differences in approach between tribunals. This uncertainty appears to be an intended consequence of the changes. The message from the Gibbons review was that 'inflexible, prescriptive regulation' had not worked and that future measures should be much simpler and more flexible but that the corollary of this was rules that would offer 'less certainty and predictability in their operation'. Gibbons' conclusion was clearly that you can't have one without the other – although it has to be said that the prescriptive SDRPs did not offer much in the way of certainty or predictability, as is evident from the huge volume of case law they generated.

Adjustment to tribunal awards

Under new S.207A(1) TULR(C)A, an employment tribunal is entitled to *increase* an award of compensation by no more than 25 per cent where:

- the claim is brought under one of the jurisdictions in Schedule A2 TULR(C)A (see Appendix 1)
- the employer has failed to comply with the Acas Code
- that failure was unreasonable, and
- the tribunal considers it just and equitable in all the circumstances to do so.

Under new S.207A(2), an employment tribunal is entitled to *reduce* an award of compensation by no more than 25 per cent where:

- the claim is brought under one of the jurisdictions in Schedule A2 TULR(C)A (see Appendix 1)
- the employee has failed to comply with the Acas Code
- that failure was unreasonable, and

8

- the tribunal considers it just and equitable in all the circumstances to do so.

In accordance with S.124A ERA (as amended by the EA 08), in an unfair dismissal case the uplift applies to the compensatory award and not to the basic award. It is applied immediately before any reduction under S.123(6) for contributory fault or under S.123(7) to offset the amount of any redundancy payment ordered by the tribunal or made by the employer that is in excess of the basic award. Where an award falls to be adjusted under S.38 of the Employment Act 2002 in respect of a failure to give a statement of employment particulars, the adjustment under S.207A should be made first – S.207A(5) TULR(C)A.

Under the old SDRPs, an award adjustment was mandatory where either party had failed to complete a relevant statutory procedure. Under the new regime, an adjustment for non compliance is *discretionary*, although the scope for tribunals to make an adjustment is much wider since they can do so if either party fails to *comply* with any of the guidance set out in the Code. Under the statutory procedures, an adjustment arose only where there had been a failure to *complete* the applicable procedure.

The power to adjust tribunal awards for a failure to comply with the Code is discusssed in greater detail in Chapter 5.

Consequential amendments

Below we set out a number of other changes that came into effect on 6 April 2009, either as a consequence of the repeal of the SDRPs or more generally to promote dispute resolution.

Automatic unfair dismissal

A failure to follow the Acas Code does not make a dismissal automatically unfair. Previously, S.98A(1) ERA – which was repealed by the EA 08 – provided that an employee who was dismissed was regarded as unfairly dismissed where the employer had not completed the statutory DDPs in respect of the employee (although the compensatory award could be reduced to reflect the likelihood that the employee would have been dismissed in any event if the statutory DDP had been complied with – the so-called 'Polkey reduction' (see below)). S.98A(2), which has also been repealed, governed the situation where the employer had not infringed the DDPs, but had otherwise failed to follow a fair procedure. That section provided that the employer's failure would not render the dismissal unfair if he could show that he would have decided to dismiss the employee in any event if he had followed the correct procedure, i.e. that the failure to follow a fair procedure had made 'no difference' to the decision to dismiss. This provision brought about a partial reversal of the principle established in Polkey v AE Dayton Services Ltd 1988

9

ICR 142, HL, that, except in exceptional circumstances where following a fair procedure would have been 'futile', a dismissal would be unfair where the employer had failed to follow a fair procedure even if the employee would still have been dismissed if the proper procedure had been complied with. However, the resulting compensatory award could be reduced to reflect the fact that dismissal would have occurred in any event, even if a fair procedure had been followed – the 'Polkey reduction'.

The repeal of S.98A has brought about the return of 'Polkey' and, except in exceptional cases, employers will no longer be able to invoke the 'no difference' argument when defending a failure to adopt a fair procedure, whether set out in the Acas Code or otherwise – for example, in the employer's disciplinary rules. However, the Polkey reduction will continue to apply. Furthermore, in cases to which the Acas Code applies, compensation may, at the tribunal's discretion, be increased by up to 25 per cent to reflect the employer's unreasonable failure to follow the Code – S.207A TULR(C)A.

The Polkey case is considered further in Chapter 5 under 'Unfair dismissal'.

TUPE

Regulation 11 of the Transfer of Undertakings (Protection of Employment) Regulations 2006 SI 2006/246 requires the transferor of a business to notify the transferee of certain employee liability information. This includes information of any relevant disciplinary procedure taken against an employee and any relevant grievance procedure taken by an employee within the previous two years. Prior to 6 April 2009, relevant procedures were those covered by the Dispute Resolution Regulations. As a result of amendment by the Transfer of Undertakings (Protection of Employment) (Amendment) Regulations 2009 SI 2009/592, relevant procedures are now those covered by the revised Acas Code of Practice.

Acas conciliation

Fixed conciliation periods that restricted the period during which Acas had a duty to assist parties to tribunal proceedings to reach a conciliated settlement were introduced in 2004 and were contained in rules 22–24 of Schedule 1 to the Employment Tribunals (Constitution and Rules of Procedure) Regulations 2004 SI 2004/1861 (the Tribunal Rules). The Government's reason for limiting the time available for Acas conciliation was to encourage parties to settle in good time rather than immediately before a tribunal hearing, thereby promoting early dispute resolution. However, in response to the Gibbons Review's conclusion that the desired effect was not being achieved, the fixed periods were repealed by Reg 4(16) of the Employment Tribunals (Constitution and Rules of Procedure) (Amendment) Regulations 2008 SI 2008/3240 as from 6 April 2009, with the effect that where Acas is under a duty to attempt to achieve conciliation, that duty now subsists throughout tribunal proceedings rather than being limited to fixed periods.

Pre-claim conciliation. At the same time, Ss.5 and 6 of the EA 08 amended S.18 of the Employment Tribunals Act 1996 to replace Acas's duty to conciliate in certain circumstances before proceedings have been instituted with a power to conciliate. In its 'Guidance note: Conciliation in cases that could be the subject of employment tribunal proceedings after 6 April 2009', Acas has stated that it will seek to make conciliation available in any dispute that is otherwise likely to be the subject of a tribunal claim, subject to the following considerations:

- the employer and employee must have already made reasonable efforts to resolve the issue(s), for instance by using the organisation's grievance or discipline procedures

- there must be grounds to believe that a valid claim is likely to be made (for example, there is a prima facie cause of action, the employee appears eligible to make the claim, and there is not already a binding agreement to settle the matter)

- where providing conciliation in potential individual rights claims could risk undermining collective and/or other agreements and procedures, it will generally be inappropriate

- if the volume of potential claims exceeds Acas's capacity, it will prioritise cases, generally focusing on those in which the employment relationship can be preserved and those which would tend to lead to longer hearings.

Initially, pre-claims conciliation will not be available in potential claims relating solely to one of the following jurisdictions:

- unlawful deduction of wages

- breach of contract

- redundancy payment

- holiday pay

as such claims can usually be quickly disposed of by tribunals. However, Acas will provide pre-claim conciliation in multiple claims covering any of the above jurisdictions where it appears there are collective employment relations implications. It hopes to broaden pre-claim conciliation to all jurisdictions by the end of 2009.

To facilitate early conciliation, Acas launched a new pre-claim conciliation service (PCC) on 6 April 2009. This is largely accessed through its Helpline (08457 47 47 47), which is available from 8 am to 8 pm Monday to Friday and 9 am to 1 pm on Saturdays. In relevant cases, a Helpline adviser will refer an issue to a conciliator where it appears to him or her that there is a potential tribunal claim.

New claim forms

The 2008 Amendment Regulations (see 'Acas conciliation' above) amend Rule 1 of the Tribunal Rules to reflect the fact that the ET1 claim form no longer requires claimants to declare their compliance with the statutory grievance procedure or to state whether they are an employee. The ET3 response form has also been revised to reflect these changes.

Failure to provide statement of employment particulars

It should be noted that one of the dispute resolution provisions introduced by the Employment Act 2002 that has survived is S.38, which provides for a financial penalty if an employer has failed to provide an employee with a written statement of employment particulars as required by S.1 ERA. Briefly, S.1 gives employees the right to a written statement of terms and conditions of employment (also referred to as 'written particulars') no later than two months after he or she starts work – see IDS Employment Law Handbook, 'Contracts of Employment' (2001), Chapter 3. That statement must include a note specifying the procedure that applies when an employee is dismissed, disciplined or brings a grievance.

Section 38 of the 2002 Act states that tribunals must award compensation to an employee where, upon a successful claim being made under any of the tribunal jurisdictions listed in Schedule 5 (see Appendix 2), it becomes evident that the employer was in breach of his duty to provide full and accurate written particulars under S.1 ERA. But note that such financial remedy is *only* available when the employee has issued proceedings on a separate matter under one of the Schedule 5 jurisdictions – and the employer was in breach of his S.1 duty at the time those proceedings were begun. There is otherwise no financial compensation available to an employee who has not been provided with a statement of employment particulars, although he or she can make a reference to an employment tribunal, which can determine what particulars should be provided. In Scott-Davies v Redgate Medical Services 2007 ICR 348 the EAT held that the fact that S.38 is also listed as one of the jurisdictions in Schedule 5 did not give the tribunal jurisdiction to hear an independent claim for compensation.

In circumstances where the claimant has succeeded in a claim listed in Schedule 5 and the employer has failed in his S.1 duty, the tribunal must award the claimant two weeks' pay unless there are exceptional circumstances that would make such an award or increase unjust or inequitable (S.38(5)). The tribunal may increase the award to four weeks' pay if it is just and equitable in all the circumstances (S.38(3)).

12

Transitional provisions

As mentioned earlier, the SDRPs did not disappear overnight on their repeal but continue to apply to disputes where the 'trigger event' occurs before the cut-off dates set out in the Employment Act 2008 (Commencement No.1, Transitional Provisions and Savings) Order 2008 SI 2008/3232. Where they do still apply, the associated three-month extension for bringing a tribunal claim, the compensation adjustments and the automatic unfair provisions will also apply. In this section we briefly explain the transitional provisions that determine whether the new or old regime applies. For a detailed discussion of the old SDRPs, reference should be had to IDS Employment Law Supplement, 'Statutory Disciplinary and Grievance Procedures' (2004).

Determining which regime applies

When the trigger event occurred before 6 April 2009, the existing procedures continue to apply. Where it occurred on or after 6 April, they do not. There are different trigger events depending on whether a grievance or a disciplinary situation arises.

Cut-off dates – grievances. The trigger for a grievance procedure will be the date of the action about which the employee complains. If the action occurred wholly before 6 April 2009, the existing GPs continue to apply. However, they also apply if the action complained of began on or before 5 April 2009 and continues beyond that date where the employee has submitted a written grievance or an employment tribunal claim (an ET1):

- on or before 4 July 2009 if it relates to a jurisdiction with a three-month time limit (as it is in most cases; for example, constructive dismissal and discrimination claims), or

- on or before 4 October 2009 if it relates to a jurisdiction with a six-month time limit (namely, equal pay or redundancy payments claims, and claims for dismissals taken in connection with industrial action under S.238 TULR(C)A).

It is unlikely that a grievance would need to be raised in connection with a dismissal under S.238 TULR(C)A since the GPs only apply to constructive dismissals and the circumstances in which a constructive dismissal occurs as a result of the employee taking industrial action are not readily apparent. However, the Department of Business, Enterprise and Regulatory Reform (BERR) says that as this is theoretically possible, it wanted to ensure that all potential scenarios, however unlikely, were covered by the transitional arrangements.

The transitional provisions mean that some claims to which the statutory GPs apply may not be heard by a tribunal until 2010. Cases that require ongoing

13

case management discussions, which are not uncommon in, for example, the equal pay arena, or those that end up on appeal, may even run into 2011.

Cut-off dates – disciplinary and dismissal cases. The trigger date for determining which regime applies to disciplinary action or dismissal will be the date when the employer has started the disciplinary or dismissal action. This will usually be the date that a Step 1 letter was sent to the employee or the date of the Step 2 meeting. If neither step has been taken, it will be the date of the disciplinary action or dismissal.

The statutory DDPs will therefore continue to apply if on or before 5 April 2009 the employer has:

- sent the employee a Step 1 statement or held a Step 2 disciplinary or dismissal meeting, or

- taken relevant disciplinary action against the employee, or

- dismissed the employee.

Under the standard procedure, the Step 1 statement must set out in writing the employee's alleged conduct, characteristics or circumstances which led the employer to contemplate dismissing or taking disciplinary action against him or her. Where the modified procedure is used, the employer must set out in writing the employee's alleged misconduct which has led to the dismissal and the basis for believing at the time of the dismissal that the employee was guilty of the alleged misconduct.

BERR has issued guidance on the application of the transitional provisions and provided example scenarios to explain which regime applies. These examples are reproduced in Appendix 3. It is inevitable that there will be a period during which parallel regimes are operating which will last into 2010 and possibly beyond.

2 Disciplinary and grievance policies

Status of policy

Agreeing policy

Policy content

As explained in the previous chapter, now that the statutory dispute resolution procedures (SDRPs) have been repealed, there is no prescribed procedure that employers and employees must follow in disciplinary and grievance situations. Instead they should comply with the standards of fairness set out in the revised Acas Code of Practice on Disciplinary and Grievance Procedures ('the Code') (available at www.acas.org.uk/drr). A failure to do so may lead to an adjustment in the amount of compensation awarded in any subsequent employment tribunal claim.

Paragraph 2 of the Acas Code states that rules and procedures for handling disciplinary and grievance situations 'should be set down in writing, be specific and clear'. Since the language of the Code is aspirational rather than prescriptive and a breach of its provisions does not in itself give rise to legal action, it is arguable that a written policy is not strictly mandatory. However, a failure to put procedures in writing risks not only an uplift in compensation in relevant cases but also a finding of unfair dismissal. It is also considered good practice to have written rules and procedures as this encourages fairness and consistency.

Furthermore, S.3 of the Employment Rights Act 1996 (ERA) requires that the statement of employment particulars that employers must provide under S.1 of that Act should include a note setting out 'any disciplinary rules' (or referring the employee to a document containing such rules) and specifying 'to whom the employee can apply for the purpose of seeking redress of any grievance'. Similarly, under S.4 ERA, any changes must be notified to employees in a written statement containing particulars of the change. The absence of any written procedures and subsequent reference to them in a statement of employment particulars will leave an employer open to a claim under S.11 ERA for failure to provide a valid S.1 statement.

Status of policy

An employer has a choice between making a disciplinary and grievance policy part of employees' contracts, subject to their agreement, or devising a free-standing policy that has no contractual basis. In workplaces where there is a

15

recognised union or relevant information and consultation agreement (see below), the employer may agree the policy with the relevant trade union or employee representatives and incorporate it into a collective agreement. We consider the three approaches below.

Contractual policy

The advantage of having a contractual policy is that employees are bound by it as well as employers and this may mean that an employee can, for example, be compelled to attend a disciplinary hearing that he or she is reluctant to take part in. The flip side is that contractual procedures do not have the same element of flexibility as non-contractual ones and any breach of the policy could lead to action for breach of contract.

Furthermore, implementing a contractual policy is more complex from a legal point of view than implementing a non-contractual one, since introducing a new policy or changing an existing one will involve a variation in employees' individual contracts of employment. Contractual variations can generally only be made in one of the following ways:

- the employer and employee may agree the change – which is what happens in the majority of cases – or the employee may by his or her conduct accept a change imposed by the employer, e.g. by carrying on working under the changed contract without protest

- individual contracts may be varied by a collective agreement which is binding on individual employees (see below, under 'Collective agreements')

- the contract itself may authorise changes

- the employer may simply terminate the existing contract and substitute a new one. This will not amount to a breach of contract if proper notice is given but may give rise to an unfair dismissal claim.

A detailed consideration of contract variation falls outside the scope of this Supplement – for full information, see IDS Employment Law Handbook, 'Contracts of Employment' (2001), Chapter 6.

Note that where a policy is incorporated into a contract of employment by reference – for example, where a term in the contract states that disciplinary issues will be dealt with under the procedures set out in a separate policy document – only those parts of the policy capable of forming contractual terms will actually become contractual. In Bristol City Council v Deadman 2007 IRLR 888, which concerned a harassment policy, the Court of Appeal held that while the investigation and grievance procedures set out by the employer's policy formed part of employees' contracts of employment, the policy's statement that all complaints would be handled 'sensitively' was not. In the Court's view, only the detailed procedures were capable of giving rise to contractual terms. The requirement of sensitivity was merely aspirational, and could not bind the employer.

Non-contractual policy

The main advantage of having a non-contractual policy is that it gives the employer flexibility to depart from the policy if he so chooses. That said, any departure that results in non-compliance with the Acas Code must be reasonable for the employer to avoid incurring a financial penalty under S.207A TULR(C)A if the employee is successful in a subsequent tribunal claim (see Chapter 5 under 'Adjustment to tribunal awards'). Employees can also depart from a non-contractual policy, but if that departure leads to an unreasonable failure to comply with the Code, any tribunal award made may be reduced by up to 25 per cent as a result.

The other advantage for employers in having a non-contractual policy is that they need not consult with employees before making any changes to it. However, this advantage is of little practical value given that any action taken against an employee for conduct he or she was unaware could lead to disciplinary action would be likely to be considered unreasonable and could make any resulting dismissal unfair.

Collective agreement

Collective agreements, usually agreed either between an employer and the relevant trade union in respect of a particular bargaining unit or nationally between employers' organisations and trade unions representing those employers' employees, have a particular status that cannot be accurately described as either contractual or non-contractual. As a general rule, a collective agreement is not legally enforceable by the parties to it. However, collective agreements can nonetheless give rise to contractual obligations in two ways. First, the contract of employment may expressly incorporate certain elements of a collective agreement, e.g. by stating that 'grievances shall be addressed under the procedure set out in Agreement X'. Secondly, incorporation may be implied in the same way that other contractual terms are implied, e.g. where there is a clear custom that terms of collective agreements are incorporated into individual contracts or where it is obvious that the parties would have agreed to incorporation when the contract was formed had they put their minds to it.

Whether a particular term has been incorporated into a contract is a question of law. This means that a party can appeal against a decision of a tribunal or lower court concerning the contractual status of a term. For example, in Hussein v Mallenash Ltd EAT 53/96 the employer's disciplinary code provided that, in the case of unsatisfactory conduct or performance, employees would receive a final written warning. H was dismissed without a final warning and brought a wrongful dismissal claim. The employer's statement of 'Conditions

17

of Employment' to which the disciplinary code was attached provided that the 'statement sets out the main particulars of the terms and conditions of employment which, in conjunction with the Grievance and Disciplinary Procedure and any working arrangements, form the Contract of Employment' between the company and the employee. The tribunal found that the disciplinary code had not been incorporated into the employment contract; the contract merely referred to it. The EAT overturned that decision on the basis that the tribunal had erred in law. It held that the code had been incorporated and that the employer was in breach of contract.

Where some or all of the terms of a collective agreement have been incorporated into individual contracts of employment, they are treated like any other contractual term and so can only be varied with the consent of both parties, according to the general principles of contract law. If, however, individual contracts of employment expressly incorporate all collective agreements in force between the employer and the recognised trade union as revised from time to time, then the making of a new agreement – or the addition of new terms, such as a disciplinary or grievance policy, to the existing agreement – will be likely to have the effect of varying the terms under which the employee is employed – see Framptons Ltd v Badger and ors EAT 0138/06 and Martland and ors v Co-Operative Insurance Society Ltd EAT 0220/07. The same applies to collective agreements that have been impliedly incorporated into individual contracts of employment. The implied acceptance that the agreement shall be legally binding holds good for the new or amended agreement unless the employees reject it.

Occasionally, collective agreements contain variation clauses which, if incorporated into contracts of employment, may be relied upon by the employer to make changes without prior consultation and agreement – see, for example, Airlie and ors v City of Edinburgh District Council 1996 IRLR 516, EAT. However, not only does this go against good industrial practice, but also any action taken against an employee for conduct he or she was unaware could lead to disciplinary action would be likely to be considered unreasonable and could make any resulting dismissal unfair.

Where disciplinary and grievance procedures fall within the scope of an information and consultation agreement under the Information and Consultation of Employees Regulations 2004 SI 2004/3426, agreement to any new or amended policy will need to be reached with the appropriate representatives. The Regulations set down rules under which employees may be entitled to negotiate an information and consultation agreement and on 6 April 2008 were extended to all organisations employing at least 50 employees. An agreement sets out the kind of matters about which elected employee representatives are entitled to receive information and give their opinions to management. Although the default list of matters under Reg 20(1) does not include disciplinary and grievance policies, there is scope for representatives and employers to agree a wider list of topics which could include disciplinary and grievance rules and procedures.

Agreeing policy

Paragraph 2 of the Acas Code of Practice states that 'employees and, where appropriate, their representatives should be involved in the development of rules and procedures' in the interests of 'fairness and transparency'. Quite what involvement is required is not known and will inevitably vary according to the size of the organisation, but note that the Code does not require agreement from employees, merely that they be 'involved'. Involvement could be as simple as e-mailing a draft policy to all employees and inviting questions. It is unusual to require the involvement of both employees *and* their representatives, since in workplaces where policy is decided through collective agreement it is usual for the employer to negotiate with representatives and the representatives to communicate with employees. However, since disciplinary rules in particular require individuals to take personal responsibility for their actions it is important that employers ensure that each employee is aware of them.

If the policy is intended to be contractual, then of course something more than involvement is required as employers must have employees' agreement to any new terms – see 'Status of policy – contractual policy' above.

Communicating the policy

Paragraph 2 of the Code also says that it is important 'to help employees and managers understand what the rules and procedures are, where they can be found and how they are to be used'. The non-statutory Acas Guide, 'Discipline and grievances at work' ('the Guide'), which is available on the Acas website (www.acas.org.uk/drr), recommends that managers at all levels receive training and states that in workplaces where there is a recognised trade union it can be useful for there to be joint training of union officials and managers. If the poor handling of procedures by a manager leads to a finding of unfair dismissal, a tribunal may be less likely to apply an uplift to the compensation award if it finds that the employer had provided the manager with such training as it considered reasonable.

It is particularly important that employees be aware of disciplinary rules and the consequences of a failure to comply with them. Action taken against an employee for conduct he or she was unaware could result in disciplinary action is likely to be considered unreasonable and could make any resulting dismissal unfair.

The Acas Guide suggests that ideally employees should be given their own printed copy of the rules or written information about how to access them, e.g. on the organisation's intranet or in their handbook, although in a small

19

organisation it may be sufficient to display the rules in a prominent place (page 12). The Guide points out that special attention should be paid to ensure that the rules are understood by any employees without recent experience of working life (for instance young people, or those returning to work after a lengthy break) and by employees whose English or reading ability is limited or who have a disability such as visual impairment.

Proper communication of the disciplinary and grievance procedures is also required by S.3 ERA, which provides that the statement of employment particulars that an employer is required to give to all employees under S.1 of that Act must include a note specifying:

- any disciplinary rules applicable to the employee or referring the employee to the provisions of a document specifying such rules which is reasonably accessible to the employee

- any procedure applicable to the taking of disciplinary decisions relating to the employee, or to a decision to dismiss the employee, or referring the employee to the provisions of a document specifying such a procedure which is reasonably accessible to the employee

- a person to whom the employee can apply if dissatisfied with any disciplinary decision relating to him or her or any decision to dismiss him or her

- a person to whom the employee can apply for the purpose of seeking redress of any grievance relating to his or her employment and the manner in which any such application should be made, and

- where there are further steps consequent on any such application, explaining those steps or referring to the provisions of a document explaining them which is reasonably accessible to the employee.

A failure to comply with these requirements can, in certain circumstances, lead to an award of compensation of up to four weeks' pay – S.38 Employment Act 2008 (see further Chapter 1 under 'Consequential amendments – failure to provide statement of employment particulars').

Employers should note that the Acas Code of Practice is not limited to dismissals and should be followed in *all* disciplinary matters regardless of whether or not dismissal is a possible consequence. Although there is no independent cause of action arising from an employer's failure to carry out a fair disciplinary procedure, or a standalone right to complain of unjustified disciplinary action, such behaviour may lead the employee to resign and bring a complaint of unfair constructive dismissal – see Chapter 5. Even if the employee does not resign at this stage, an employment tribunal can take the fairness of the disciplinary action into account if it is later relied upon by the employer to dismiss the employee for further alleged misconduct – Digby v East Cambridgeshire District Council EAT 0522/06. Furthermore, if the employer's actions are tainted by discrimination, the employee will be entitled to bring an independent claim to an employment tribunal and any procedural failures may impact on any compensation awarded.

Related policies

Although disciplinary and grievance policies are broad-ranging, organisations may wish to have additional policies to deal with specific issues – for example, the Foreword to the Acas Code suggests that employers may wish to deal with bullying, harassment or whistleblowing under a separate procedure. Whether this is appropriate will depend on the size and structure of the business. We set out below typical policies that employers may wish to consider.

Computer-use policy. It is common practice for employers to have a computer-use policy in place, defining what is considered acceptable use of computers and e-mail facilities, particularly by reference to the downloading or sending of inappropriate or obscene content. This can be helpful for two reasons. First, if an employer wishes to take disciplinary action against an employee for unacceptable computer use, it must be clear to the employee what is and is not unacceptable. A separate policy can explain this in some detail. Secondly, an employer who has made it clear through the implementation of such a policy that e-mails containing remarks, jokes, images, etc that are offensive on one of the protected grounds of discrimination (race, sex, disability, religion or belief, sexual orientation, or age) are prohibited may have a defence to a resulting discrimination claim (although note that having such a policy does not excuse a failure to act on a specific complaint) – see Chapter 5.

Diversity/equal opportunities policy. The main purpose of an equal opportunities or diversity policy is to set out the employer's commitment to eliminating discrimination on any of the grounds set out in the policy in all aspects of the employment relationship including, among other things, recruitment and promotion, pay and the award of benefits. Such a policy might, therefore, include procedures for conducting interviews and assessments so as to eliminate the possibility of conscious or subconscious bias, provision for monitoring diversity within the organisation, and a commitment to reviewing pay so as to ensure that pay levels are not influenced by discriminatory factors. The policy might also include a statement of intent and procedures for dealing with unlawful harassment.

Bullying and harassment policy. It is possible to address bullying and harassment through existing disciplinary and grievance procedures by including a definition of such behaviour and specifying that it is unacceptable and may lead to sanctions, up to and including dismissal. However, a separate policy may give employees confidence that such issues will be dealt with sensitively and encourage them to come forward at an early stage, thereby enabling employers to nip the problem in the bud. In addition, a well-publicised and effectively implemented bullying and harassment policy is a means of discharging an employer's legal duty to protect employees against such behaviour. For more on bullying and harassment policies, see IDS Employment Law Supplement. 'Bullying and Harassment at Work' (2007).

Whistleblowing policy. There are a number of reasons why employers may wish to encourage their employees to raise concerns about suspected wrongdoings in accordance with a whistleblowing policy, not least because it helps to create a culture of openness in which employees have confidence that their concerns will be addressed. This in turn makes it less likely that workers will report their concerns to an outside body or individual and gives the employer the opportunity to investigate the alleged wrongdoing and, if necessary, put it right. A whistleblowing procedure that has been effectively implemented also reduces the risk that such a complaint will be mishandled and consequently of the employer incurring liability in a subsequent tribunal claim.

The purpose of a whistleblowing procedure is not for individuals to pursue grievances or to challenge practices with which they disagree but to provide a way in which concerns about malpractice or impropriety can be raised, and this should be made clear. These issues are discussed in detail in IDS Employment Law Supplement, 'Whistleblowing at Work' (2004).

Policy content

Disciplinary rules

A disciplinary policy should set out written rules that communicate the standards of behaviour expected within an organisation and the consequences of failing to comply with them. As the Acas Guide points out, clear rules 'set standards of conduct' and 'help employers to act fairly and consistently' (page 11). This is particularly important where there may be ambiguity about whether conduct is acceptable in a particular workplace. Dismissals have been found to be unfair because the employee had not been made aware that particular conduct was unacceptable or of the consequences of such conduct. For example, in Royal Bank of Scotland v Goudie EAT 0693/03 an employee was found to have been unfairly dismissed for misuse of her employer's computer facilities after sending an e-mail the employer considered pornographic because employees had not been told how acceptable e-mail content was graded or the sanctions that would be applied.

Although pointing out that different organisations will have different requirements, the Acas Guide suggests at page 12 that rules could cover such matters as:

- timekeeping
- absence

- health and safety

- use of the organisation's facilities

- discrimination, bullying and harassment

- personal appearance

- the types of conduct that might be considered gross misconduct (see further below).

On the basis that rules are more likely to be effective if they are seen as reasonable by those to whom they apply, the Guide considers it good practice to develop rules in consultation with employees (and, where appropriate, their representatives) and those who will be responsible for applying them – see further 'Agreeing the policy' above. It also recommends that the same rules should apply to all employees at all levels within the organisation unless there are reasons why different sets of rules should apply to different groups. Rules should be non-discriminatory. If they discriminate on any of the protected grounds of sex, transgender, marital or civil partnership status, race, sexual orientation, religion or belief, disability or age they can give rise to a discrimination claim – see Chapter 5.

Gross misconduct. Paragraph 23 of the Acas Code states that the disciplinary rules should give examples of what the employer regards as gross misconduct. This is misconduct that is seen as serious enough to justify summary dismissal (i.e. dismissal without notice), which the Code suggests might include theft or fraud, physical violence, gross negligence or serious insubordination. Although there are some types of misconduct that may be universally seen as gross misconduct, such as theft or violence, others may vary according to the nature of the organisation and what it does. In workplaces with significant health and safety risks, for example, any breach of a health and safety procedure may be viewed as gross misconduct justifying dismissal, whereas a similar breach in a workplace where workers are not exposed to the same level of risk may warrant only a warning. If an employer views certain behaviour as very serious and capable of amounting to gross misconduct because of the nature of the business but that behaviour might not be viewed in the same way elsewhere, it is particularly important to include it in the disciplinary rules so that employees are aware of that fact.

The Acas Guide gives the following examples at page 31 of gross misconduct that might be included:

- theft or fraud

- physical violence or bullying

- deliberate and serious damage to property

- serious misuse of an organisation's property or name

- deliberately accessing internet sites containing pornographic, offensive or obscene material

- serious insubordination

- unlawful discrimination or harassment

- bringing the organisation into serious disrepute

- serious incapability at work brought on by alcohol or illegal drugs

- causing loss, damage or injury though serious negligence

- a serious breach of health and safety rules

- a serious breach of confidence.

Even though gross misconduct may justify summary dismissal, an employer suspecting an employee of such conduct should still follow a fair procedure, including an investigation of the facts. If an employer does establish a reasonable belief that the employee is guilty of the misconduct in question, he must still hold a meeting and hear the employee's case, including any mitigating circumstances that might lead to a lesser sanction.

Disciplinary and grievance procedures

Unless the matter is serious, employers and employees should attempt to resolve issues that could give rise to disciplinary action or grievances informally and in many cases this will be achieved. However, procedures should set out when formal action will be taken and what its consequences will be. Note that formal action carries with it a worker's right to be accompanied, whereas informal action does not – see Chapter 6.

The Acas Code states that what kind of formal action is reasonable or justified will depend on the particular circumstances, referring in particular to the employer's size and resources, and specifies that 'it may sometimes not be practicable for all employers to take all of the steps' set out in the Code – see para 3. However, freedom to depart from a particular step has to be balanced against the need for consistency and for procedures to be specific and clear. Whatever procedures are adopted, they must comply with the general principles of fairness set out at para 4 of the Code, which apply to both disciplinary and grievance procedures. They are that:

- employers and employees should raise and deal with issues *promptly* and should not unreasonably delay meetings, decisions or confirmation of those decisions

- employers and employees should act *consistently*

- employers should carry out any necessary *investigations* to establish the facts of the case

- employers should *inform* employees of the basis of the problem and give them an opportunity to *put their case* in response before any decisions are made

- employers should allow employees to be *accompanied* at any formal disciplinary or grievance meeting

- employers should allow an employee to *appeal* against any formal decision made.

The Code also recommends the following steps for handling disciplinary and grievance issues in the workplace:

- disciplinary action

  - establish the facts of each case

  - inform the employee of the problem

  - hold a meeting with the employee to discuss the problem

  - allow the employee to be accompanied at the meeting

  - decide on appropriate action

  - provide employees with an opportunity to appeal

- grievances

  - let the employer know the nature of the grievance

  - hold a meeting with the employee to discuss the grievance

  - allow the employee to be accompanied at the meeting

  - decide on appropriate action

  - allow the employee to take the grievance further if not resolved.

Both the general principles and the key steps set out above are part of the statutory Code, which means that an unreasonable failure to follow them risks incurring liability and/or an adjustment to any compensation award in related tribunal proceedings. These requirements are discussed further in Chapters 3 and 4.

Sample procedures

Acas has provided useful sample procedures in Appendix 2 of the Guide. It offers two alternative disciplinary procedures (one for 'any organisation' and one for a 'small organisation') but just one sample grievance procedure for use in a small organisation.

3 Disciplinary action and dismissal

Conduct and capability

Sickness absence

Redundancy

Expiry of fixed-term contract

Other dismissals

The power to increase awards under new S.207A of the Trade Union and Labour Relations (Consolidation) Act 1992 (TULR(C)A) for an unreasonable failure to comply with the revised Acas Code of Practice on Disciplinary and Grievance Procedures ('the Code') only applies to claims brought under one of the jurisdictions listed in Schedule A2 to the TULR(C)A (see Appendix 1) and where 'a *relevant* Code of Practice applies' (our stress). As the Code 'is designed to help employers, employees and their representatives deal with disciplinary and grievance situations in the workplace' (see para 1), it is only really relevant in cases involving discipline and grievance matters. Even then, the significance of non-compliance with the Code's disciplinary guidelines generally arises only where an employee has been dismissed and the disciplinary proceedings come under scrutiny in a resulting tribunal claim. This is because there is no free-standing cause of action that results from an employer's failure to carry out a fair disciplinary procedure, or a standalone right to complain of unjustified disciplinary action (except in situations where that action amounts to a constructive dismissal or offends other substantive employment rights, e.g. under discrimination legislation, for which see Chapter 5).

The Code does not define 'disciplinary situations' except to say that they 'include misconduct and/or poor performance' (para 1). It specifically excludes from its scope redundancy dismissals and the non-renewal of fixed-term contracts on their expiry. This leaves a number of situations that can potentially lead to dismissal which may or may not be covered by the Code.

In this chapter we begin by explaining the procedures that should be followed in relation to conduct and capability matters in order to comply both with the Code and with the concept of reasonableness as formulated by the case law on unfair dismissal. We then consider the procedural steps that apply when dealing with sickness absence (which arguably falls outside the Code), before turning to deal with redundancy and the non-renewal of fixed-term contracts, which are specifically excluded. Finally, we discuss other situations that are not

26

considered 'disciplinary' in a strict sense but which can nevertheless lead to dismissal under one of the potentially fair grounds set out in the Employment Rights Act 1996 (ERA); namely, retirement, statutory ban and 'some other substantial reason'.

Formal or informal action. There is no statutory obligation on employers to attempt to resolve issues informally or through mediation, although it is recommended in both the Foreword to the Code and the accompanying Acas Guide 'Discipline and grievances at work' ('the Guide') (neither of which form part of the statutory Code). The Guide says that unless the situation giving rise to disciplinary action is of a serious nature, informal action will normally be considered the first step in resolving an issue and many potential disciplinary issues can be resolved in this way (page 10). Informal action will be suitable, for example, when dealing with minor misconduct or unsatisfactory performance or attendance and will usually involve a conversation between the employee and his or her line manager, with the aim of encouraging improvement.

While the Acas Guide warns against informal action inadvertently turning into formal disciplinary action, it also suggests that if improvement is required the employer should make sure that the employee understands 'how their performance or conduct will be reviewed, and over what period', and that it may be useful to set out in writing what has been decided (page 11). One word of caution: since notions of 'informality' differ, employers should be aware that if the outcome of such discussions, however informal the employer considers them to be, is a warning with a set time limit or is taken into account in subsequent disciplinary action, this is likely be viewed by a tribunal as formal action. One of the dangers here is that the employer may have denied the employee his or her statutory right to be accompanied to a formal disciplinary hearing – see, for example, London Underground Ltd v Ferenc-Batchelor; Harding v London Underground Ltd 2003 ICR 656, EAT. (Note that the right to be accompanied is dealt with in Chapter 6.)

Conduct and capability

As mentioned above, the Acas Code expressly covers disciplinary issues relating to misconduct and poor performance, both of which are potentially fair reasons for dismissal under the ERA: the former on grounds of 'conduct' under S.98(2)(b); the latter on grounds of 'capability or qualifications' under S.98(2)(a). However, the category 'capability or qualifications' encompasses more than simply poor performance, and it is less clear how the Code applies to the broader issues of incapability on grounds of sickness absence or lack of qualification that are embraced by it. These grounds for dismissal are considered further in the relevant sections below. However, we first examine

27

the six steps set out in the Acas Code that are the 'keys to handling disciplinary issues in the workplace', and which employers must normally follow if they are to comply with the Code. These steps are:

- establish the facts of each case (paras 5–8)

- inform the employee of the problem (paras 9–10)

- hold a meeting with the employee to discuss the problem (paras 11–12)

- allow the employee to be accompanied at the meeting (paras 13–16)

- decide on appropriate action (paras 17–24)

- provide employees with an opportunity to appeal (paras 25–28).

All references to paragraph numbers in this section are to the Code.

Gross misconduct. The Code states that 'a fair disciplinary process should always be followed before dismissing for gross misconduct' (para 22). Thus, unless the misconduct is so heinous as to require instant dismissal – e.g. where there is a danger to life or immediate severe harm to the business – even serious conduct cases should be dealt with in the normal way. (Where immediate dismissal is deemed necessary, it is arguable that the lack of a fair procedure would not render it unfair as the exception in Polkey v AE Dayton Services Ltd 1988 ICR 142, HL, would apply. This exception – which provides that a proper procedure can be dispensed with where it would have been 'utterly useless' or 'futile' in the circumstances – is discussed in Chapter 5 under 'Unfair dismissal'. But even if the dismissal was found to be unfair, a tribunal might find that the failure to comply with the Code was reasonable in the circumstances and that it would not be just and equitable to make an uplift to any award of compensation – see further Chapter 5 under 'Adjustment to tribunal awards'.)

Establish the facts

An employer should carry out an investigation to establish the facts before he takes any disciplinary action, although the extent of that investigation and the form that it takes will vary according to the particular circumstances. Not only is an investigation required under the Code, but case law demonstrates that a failure to carry out a reasonable investigation will make a resulting dismissal unfair. Indeed, it has long been established as one of the essential requirements of a fair conduct dismissal – see British Homes Stores Ltd v Burchell 1980 ICR 303, EAT.

The investigation should be carried out without unreasonable delay, although it is not essential that it take the form of an investigatory meeting with the employee. While a meeting may be appropriate in some cases, in others the investigation stage may only involve the employer collating evidence (para 5).

An investigatory meeting should not result in disciplinary action (para 7). If it becomes clear during the course of such a meeting that disciplinary action is needed, the meeting should be adjourned and the employee given notice of a separate disciplinary hearing and told of his or her right to be accompanied. As explained in Chapter 6, an employee has a statutory right to be accompanied at a disciplinary hearing but not an investigatory meeting, unless this is allowed by the employer's own procedure.

Even in cases of gross misconduct employers should be slow to conclude that an investigation is unnecessary. Two contrasting examples:

- **Boys and Girls Welfare Society v McDonald** 1997 ICR 693, EAT: McD was employed as a residential social worker in a children's home. During an altercation, he spat at one of the children. He admitted doing so at the disciplinary hearing and was dismissed. Since there was no real conflict on the facts, it was not necessary for M's employer to interview the boy with whom McD had the altercation or to consider the extreme provocation under which McD was placed

- **Scottish Daily Record and Sunday Mail (1986) Ltd v Laird** 1996 IRLR 665, Ct Sess (Inner House): L was dismissed for failing to inform his employer of some outside professional interests. Although there was no dispute that he should have informed his employer of these other interests and had not done so, the Court stated that an investigation should nonetheless have taken place because there was a dispute as to whether there was a conflict between G's job with the employer and his other professional interests.

An employer who fails to establish all the facts risks a finding that a resulting dismissal was unfair both for a failure to carry out a reasonable investigation and a failure to comply with the Acas Code, which carries an attendant risk that any compensation payable will be increased by up to 25 per cent.

Impartiality. Employers should keep an open mind when carrying out an investigation. If disciplinary action results in dismissal and there is an indication that the employer has pre-judged the outcome, that can be enough to make the dismissal unfair. For example, in Sovereign Business Integration plc v Trybus EAT 0107/07 the EAT found that there had been an inadequate investigation resulting in an unfair dismissal when the employer had preconceptions that coloured the whole process.

Paragraph 6 of the Code states that, in misconduct cases, 'where practicable, different people should carry out the investigation and disciplinary hearing'. Such a division of functions is recognised by the courts as an important indicator of impartiality. An example:

- **Warren James Jewellers Ltd v Christy** EAT 1041/02: C was dismissed on suspicion of theft when the bank paying-in slip for a day when she was left in charge of the shop was short by £1,000. In holding that her dismissal was unfair, the employment tribunal found that there had been no reasonable

29

investigation, pointing to the fact that, among other things, the area manager who acted as the investigation officer was also responsible for disciplining and dismissing C. In upholding the tribunal's decision, the EAT referred to Lord Justice Mummery's statement in J Sainsbury plc v Hitt 2003 ICR 111, CA, that: 'The range of reasonable responses test (or, to put it another way, the need to apply the objective standards of the reasonable employer) applies as much to the question whether the investigation into the suspected misconduct was reasonable in all the circumstances as it does to the reasonableness of the decision to dismiss for the conduct reason.'

The same principle of impartiality extends to those acting as witnesses in an investigation. For example:

- **Moyes v Hylton Castle Working Men's Social Club and Institute Ltd** 1986 IRLR 482, EAT: M was dismissed from his job as club steward after two incidents in which he allegedly sexually harassed a barmaid, the second of which was observed by the chairman and the assistant secretary of the club. The investigation was carried out by a sub-committee of five, which included the two club officials who were witnesses. A subsequent meeting of the full committee, which again included the chairman and assistant secretary, made the decision to dismiss. Overturning the employment tribunal's decision that the involvement of the two officials in the capacity of both witness and judge did not make the dismissal unfair, the EAT held that this was a breach of natural justice and any reasonable observer would conclude that justice did not appear to have been done and had not been done. The EAT acknowledged that there could be cases where a witness to an incident would have to make the decision to dismiss but in the present case found that it was entirely unnecessary for the two officials to act in both roles.

However, as the EAT accepted in the Moyes case, it is not always possible in small organisations for functions to be separated in this way. In Barlow v Clifford and Co (Sidcup) Ltd EAT 0910/04 the EAT found that where there are a limited number of people available it is not necessarily unfair for the same people to be involved in the early stages of the disciplinary process and in the decision to dismiss.

In conducting the investigation, an employer should interview witnesses, although he need not interview every available witness once a fact has been clearly established. However, the investigation may be unsatisfactory if an obvious witness is overlooked. For example, where the employer relied on a second-hand account of a fight between two employees instead of interviewing the only eye-witness, the investigation was found to be flawed – Baxters (Butchers) Ltd v Hart EAT 934/83. As explained below, an employee may be allowed to call witnesses to a disciplinary hearing.

30

More than one suspect. Where one of two employees is suspected of being responsible for acts or omissions meriting dismissal and the employer, despite reasonable investigation, cannot discover which of them is to blame, it may be fair to dismiss both. This rule was established by the Court of Appeal in Monie v Coral Racing Ltd 1981 ICR 109 – a case of suspected theft where more than one employee was under suspicion but the culprit was unidentifiable – and has been followed in a range of other circumstances. For example, where one of two employees was to blame for fighting – British Aerospace v Mafe EAT 565/80, and where damage was due to faulty servicing by one of two workers – McPhie and anor v Wimpey Waste Management Ltd 1981 IRLR 316, EAT. However, it is not applied lightly and in Leyland Vehicles Ltd v Wright EAT 712/81 the EAT made it clear that suspicion must have been narrowed to the point of certainty that it was one of two employees who was guilty of the act complained of. In that case, there was 'no reasonable conclusive proof' that one of the two dismissed employees must have been guilty of theft.

Note that if the investigation does establish a genuine belief in the employer's mind that more than one person is guilty of misconduct the employer must still consider the individual circumstances of each employee when deciding on what action is appropriate – Paul v East Surrey District Health Authority 1995 IRLR 305 (see 'Consistency of treatment' below).

Suspension. In some circumstances an employer may feel it necessary to suspend the employee while the investigation is being carried out and until any disciplinary action takes place. However, if a suspension with pay is considered necessary it should be as brief as possible and kept under review and it should be made clear to the employee that the suspension does not amount to disciplinary action (para 8).

Suspension without pay will be in breach of contract unless there is a clear contractual term allowing it.

Inform the employee
If, once the investigation has been completed, disciplinary action is considered necessary, the employer should inform the employee in writing of the charge(s) against him or her and the possible consequences of the disciplinary action (para 9). This should contain enough information to enable him or her to prepare an answer to the case. The Code states that it would normally be appropriate to provide copies of any written evidence, including witness statements. The notification should also give details of the time and venue for the disciplinary hearing (para 10).

Employee must know full allegations against him or her. There are many examples of cases in which a failure to inform an employee of the full allegations against him or her has led to a finding of unfair dismissal. Two examples:

- **Hotson v Wisbech Conservative Club** 1984 ICR 859, EAT: the stated reason for the dismissal of a club barmaid was gross inefficiency in handling bar takings. During the tribunal hearing of her unfair dismissal complaint the chairman suggested, and the employer's representative agreed, that the employer was really alleging dishonesty. The tribunal proceeded to find the dismissal fair on the ground of suspected dishonesty. The EAT held that the difference between inefficiency and dishonesty was more than a mere change of label. The charge of dishonesty should have been stated at the outset or not stated at all: at the very least the employee should have had the fullest opportunity to consider the implications of the charge and to answer it

- **Murphy v Epsom College** 1985 ICR 80, CA: M was dismissed on the ground of redundancy. A tribunal found that this was a fair dismissal either for redundancy or for 'some other substantial reason', although the employer had never argued the latter as a ground for dismissal before the tribunal. The EAT agreed that this was a fair dismissal for redundancy, but said that the tribunal should not have found 'some other substantial reason' as this had neither been pleaded nor expressly raised at the tribunal. M appealed further. The Court of Appeal held that the EAT had been correct in finding a fair dismissal for redundancy and also in holding that natural justice requires that no party should have a case decided against them on a ground on which they have not had an opportunity to be heard.

Allow the employee to be accompanied

When informing the employee of the time and venue for the disciplinary meeting, the employer should advise the employee of his or her right to be accompanied (para 10). This right is explained fully in Chapter 6.

Hold a meeting

The disciplinary hearing should be held 'without unreasonable delay whilst allowing the employee reasonable time to prepare their case' (para 11). An employee has a statutory right to ask for a meeting to be rescheduled if necessary in order for his or her chosen companion to attend as long as the alternative date suggested is within five working days of that proposed by the employer (see Chapter 6). Employers and employees (and their companions) should make every effort to attend the meeting (para 12).

Before the meeting, the employer should notify the employee in writing that there is a disciplinary case to answer and this should contain sufficient information about the alleged misconduct or poor performance and its possible consequences to enable the employee to prepare to answer the case at a disciplinary meeting (para 9). As stated above, it would normally be appropriate to provide copies of any written evidence, which may include any witness statements, at this stage.

The Acas Guide recommends that employers arrange for someone who is not involved in the case to attend the meeting to take a note and act as a witness to what was said (page 19). If the employee needs an interpreter or facilitator because of a language barrier or understanding difficulties, the Guide suggests that the employer consider providing one. The attendance of an individual in this role may be in addition to the employee's companion. Although the Guide says that 'ideally one person should carry out both roles', this will not necessarily be practical and employers should always remember that the overriding test in a case of unfair dismissal is one of reasonableness in the circumstances. Note that if the employee has a disability and needs an interpreter or other assistant at the meeting in order to remove any disadvantage faced by the employee as a result of that disability, an employer's refusal to allow one may be a breach of his duty to make reasonable adjustments under the Disability Discrimination Act 1995 (see Chapter 5).

Conduct of meeting. Para 12 of the Code sets out the following requirements:

- the employer should explain the complaint against the employee and go through the evidence that has been gathered

- the employee should be allowed to set out his or her case and answer any allegations that have been made

- the employee should be given a reasonable opportunity to ask questions, present evidence and call witnesses

- the employee should be given an opportunity to raise points about any information provided by witnesses

- where an employer or employee intends to call relevant witnesses they should give advance notice that they intend to do this.

The Guide points out that the purpose of the meeting is to establish the facts rather than to catch people out, and suggests that it contain the following five elements:

- statement of the complaint by the employer outlining the complaint and the evidence

- employee's reply answering any allegations that have been made

- general questioning and discussion, which should be a two-way process

- summing up

- adjournment before a decision (pages 20-22).

Absence of bias. It is a principle of natural justice that the person conducting the proceedings should not be a 'judge in his own cause'. In other words, the decision-maker should not have a direct interest in the outcome of the proceedings and should not give any appearance of bias or partiality.

Commonly cited evidence of bias is where a supervisor or manager involved in the disciplinary proceedings was also involved at an earlier stage in the case and so may already have formed an opinion. In order to minimise the possibility of bias the procedure should separate the processes of investigation, decision-making and appeal wherever possible. In Whitbread plc (t/a Whitbread Medway Inns) v Hall 2001 ICR 699, CA, the dismissal of H was found to be unfair despite his admission of guilt because the manager holding the disciplinary meeting had initiated the investigation and was biased against him, as she had already made up her mind to dismiss.

Non-attendance of employee. Paragraph 24 of the Code states that 'where an employee is persistently unable or unwilling to attend a disciplinary meeting without good cause the employer should make a decision on the evidence available'. There are obvious areas for dispute here over the definitions of 'persistently' and 'without good cause' and employers should exercise caution before proceeding with a disciplinary hearing in the employee's absence.

Before making a decision on how to proceed when an employee is repeatedly unable or unwilling to attend a meeting, the Acas Guide suggests that the employer take into account the following considerations:

- any rules the organisation has for dealing with failure to attend disciplinary meetings

- the seriousness of the disciplinary issue under consideration

- the employee's disciplinary record (including current warnings), general work record, work experience, position and length of service

- medical opinion on whether the employee is fit to attend the meeting

- how similar cases in the past have been dealt with (page 20).

In the following case the employer acted unfairly by jumping to conclusions about an employee's fitness to attend a meeting:

- **William Hicks and Partners (A Firm) v Nadal** EAT 0164/05: N was suspended over a number of allegations including bullying and intimidation of staff and a couple of days later her doctor wrote to the employer to say that she was suffering from stress and was not fit to attend any hearing in the foreseeable future. Despite this the employer arranged a disciplinary hearing, but it was postponed on a couple of occasions following the receipt of further sick notes. Eventually, however, the hearing took place in N's absence after the employer discovered that she had been in negotiations with a new employer. The EAT upheld the tribunal's finding of unfair dismissal on the grounds that N's employer should not have ignored medical advice it had commissioned without 'compelling evidence' that N was 'pulling the wool over her own doctor's eyes' or in the absence of 'authoritative contrary medical evidence' about her fitness, neither of which it had. The EAT pointed out that the opportunity for an employee to put his or her side of matters had long been established as an essential part of a reasonable investigation. It accepted that there may be cases where an employer had made proper enquires, including sufficient medical enquiries, to establish that the employee was fit to attend a hearing but had unreasonably declined to do so without just cause. However, it said this must be an exception to the general rule that disciplinary hearings should always involve the presence of the employee.

In Burns v Turboflex Ltd EAT 377/96 the EAT emphasised that employers should allow employees to answer allegations of poor performance. In that case the claimant was dismissed while he was out of the country. The EAT held that it was contrary to the rules of natural justice to deny him the chance to respond to the allegations made against him.

Witnesses. The inclusion in para 12 of the Code of a right to call witnesses has raised some eyebrows, not least because case law is more ambiguous on this point. In Santamera v Express Cargo Forwarding t/a IEC Ltd 2003 IRLR 273 the EAT held that an employment tribunal had been entitled to find that an employer who refused to allow an employee to cross-examine colleagues who had made allegations of misconduct against her had nevertheless carried out a reasonable investigation into the employee's alleged wrongdoing and, following that investigation, had dismissed her fairly. However, although the rules on fairness contained in S.98(4) ERA do not require an employer to carry out 'a forensic or quasi-judicial investigation', it did not follow that an employer will never be obliged to allow an employee to cross-examine his or her accusers during disciplinary proceedings. The EAT emphasised that in each case a tribunal must decide with reference to the facts before it whether the employer's procedure had been fair and reasonable. The decision leaves open the question of when it is reasonable for an employer to allow cross-examination of witnesses and when it is not. Its effect is that, so long as a refusal to allow cross-examination falls within the band of reasonable responses open to the employer, it will not render a dismissal unfair.

Admittedly, the Code does not specifically state that employees have the right to cross-examine witnesses, merely to call them. However, there would be little point in calling a witness to attend a hearing if questions could not be put to him or her and it has to be assumed that the intention behind the Code is to allow witnesses to be questioned. It is, of course, open to an employer to refuse to allow a witness to be called if it is reasonable in the circumstances, although there is no guidance as to what would be considered reasonable here. The rules of natural justice, in so far as they apply to disciplinary hearings, require that an employee know precisely what the accusations against him or her are and have a full opportunity of stating his or her case. It seems appropriate,

35

therefore, that the question of whether or not it is reasonable to allow a witness to be called in a particular case should be decided in light of these principles.

If an allegation has been made by, or evidence obtained from, an individual who is not an employee of the employer's organisation, such as a customer, it may not be practicable or desirable for that person to attend a disciplinary hearing. In such cases, the Guide recommends that the employer try to get a written statement from that individual (page 19). If a witness – whether or not a fellow employee – wants to remain anonymous, the Guide advises employers to take written statements, seek corroborative evidence, and check that the person's motives are genuine.

Guidance for employers wishing to rely on evidence from someone who wishes to remain anonymous was provided by the EAT in Linfood Cash and Carry Ltd v Thomson and anor 1989 ICR 518. In trying to maintain a balance of interest between protecting the anonymity of the informant and providing a fair hearing for the employee, the EAT made the following suggestions:

- informants' statements should be reduced to writing (although they might need to be edited later to preserve anonymity)

- in taking statements it is important to note the date, time and place of each observation or incident; the informant's opportunity to observe clearly and accurately; circumstantial evidence, such as knowledge of a system, the reason for the informant's presence or any memorable small details; and whether the informant had any reason to fabricate evidence

- further investigation should then take place, corroboration being clearly desirable

- tactful inquiries into the character and background of the informant would be advisable

- a decision must then be taken whether to hold a disciplinary hearing, particularly when the employer is satisfied that the informant's fear is genuine

- if the disciplinary process is to continue, the responsible member of management at each stage of the procedure should personally interview the informant and decide what weight is to be given to his or her evidence

- the informant's written statement – if necessary with omissions to avoid identification – should be made available to the employee and his or her representative

- if the employee or his or her representative raises an issue that should be put to the informant, it may be desirable to adjourn the disciplinary proceedings so that the chairman can question the informant

- it is particularly important that full and careful notes be taken at disciplinary hearings when informants are involved

- if evidence from an investigating officer is to be taken at a hearing it should where possible be prepared in writing. (Note that this final point is not limited to cases where an investigation has been started because of statements made by an informant.)

However, as the EAT itself noted: 'Every case must depend upon its own facts, and circumstances may vary widely.' In Ramsey and ors v Walkers Snack Foods Ltd and anor 2004 IRLR 754 the Linford guidelines were not followed fully. In particular, full statements were not taken from informants at the outset and the statements that were taken were heavily edited. In addition, informants were only interviewed by one manager, who was not involved in the disciplinary process. However, the EAT noted that the case involved multiple informants who were terrified of being identified because they worked in a factory with a close-knit community. They were thus unwilling to sign statements unless they had been sufficiently edited so as to remove any risk of identification. Nor did they wish to be exposed to further questioning that might risk their identities becoming known. In the circumstances, the risk of reprisals was real. The EAT stated that, when considering whether or not the approach taken was fair, the focus should be on the reasons for granting anonymity in the first place. On this basis, as the tribunal had made a clear finding that the offer of anonymity was reasonable and the employer genuinely believed that no information would be provided unless it was entirely confidential, the approach taken was fair, notwithstanding non-compliance with the Linford guidelines in some respects.

An employer will not always be able to guarantee the anonymity of an informant, however. In A v Company B Ltd 1997 IRLR 405, ChD, A's reputation in the industry in which he worked was destroyed when accusations were made against him by an anonymous informant. His employer, despite having lost a claim of unfair dismissal, refused to disclose either the nature of the allegations against him or the identity of the informant. As A was not in a position to counter the allegations, he was unable to repair his reputation and therefore unable to find a new job. The High Court granted his application for an order requiring B Ltd to reveal both the nature of the allegations and the identity of his accuser. The Court decided that it had discretion to order the disclosure of an informant's identity where this was necessary to enable an employee to know whether he had a civil action for defamation or malicious falsehood against the person whose information led to the employee's dismissal. It was intolerable, the Court said, that an individual could be stained by serious allegations, the nature of which he had no means of discovering, and be left in a position where he could not even invoke the law to defend his reputation.

Grievance raised during disciplinary procedure. The Code of Practice recommends (at para 44) that where an employee raises a grievance during a disciplinary process the disciplinary process may need to be temporarily suspended in order to deal with the matter. However, where the grievance and disciplinary cases are related, it may be appropriate to deal with both issues concurrently. The Code clearly intends employers to have a discretion to deal with the situation appropriately that was not available to them under the statutory disciplinary procedures. The accompanying Guide suggests that a suspension of the disciplinary procedure may be appropriate where:

- the grievance relates to a conflict of interest that the manager holding the disciplinary meeting is alleged to have

- bias is alleged in the conduct of the disciplinary meeting

- management have been selective in the evidence they have supplied to the manager holding the meeting

- there is possible discrimination (page 22).

Decide on appropriate action

It is good practice for the employer to adjourn the disciplinary hearing in order to consider the case before coming to a decision. The Acas Code states that 'after the meeting' the employer should decide whether or not disciplinary or any other action is justified and inform the employee accordingly in writing (para 17).

In deciding whether disciplinary action is appropriate and, if so, what form it should take, the Acas Guide suggests that employers consider:

- whether the rules of the organisation indicate what the likely penalty will be as a result of the particular misconduct

- the penalty imposed in similar cases in the past

- whether standards of other employees are acceptable, and whether this employee is not being unfairly singled out

- the employee's disciplinary record (including current warnings), general work record, work experience, position and length of service

- any special circumstances which might make it appropriate to adjust the severity of the penalty

- whether the proposed penalty is reasonable in all the circumstances

- whether any training, additional support or adjustments to the work are necessary (page 27).

Length of service. The employee's length of service is relevant when deciding the appropriate sanction. In Strouthos v London Underground Ltd 2004 IRLR

636, CA, the Court held that the fact that S had been employed for 20 years with no relevant previous warnings was material. While acknowledging that there can be conduct so serious that dismissal is appropriate irrespective of length of service, the EAT had been wrong to say that length of service was not relevant.

Prior disciplinary record. Where a previous warning has been given the employer should take into account the employee's progress during the improvement period. In Schuckle v Martin Ford Ltd COET 610/34 one of the factors leading to a finding of unfair dismissal was that during the improvement period the employee had made substantial progress which the company did not make itself aware of. And the fact that an employee has shown at least *some* capacity to improve may be taken into account by a tribunal when determining whether the dismissal of an employee for failing to make sufficient improvement falls within the band of reasonable responses. In Tufail v Scottish Life Assurance Co ET Case No.28133/95, for example, a tribunal was critical of the employer's decision to dismiss the claimant for lack of capability given that she had responded positively to a previous warning regarding her performance. The claimant in that case had begun working for the employer in 1987 and had had a satisfactory record until 1993, when she was transferred to a new department. Her annual appraisal for 1994 graded her work as unsatisfactory, as a result of which she was given a written warning. Two months after that, her Divisional Manager reported that her standard of work had improved to the extent that he was now satisfied with her performance. At her next appraisal her work was again graded as unsatisfactory and she was given another warning – this time described as being a 'first and final warning'. Her performance was then monitored weekly. The employer's assessment was that, while her performance had improved, the degree of improvement was not sufficient to bring her up to the required standard and she was dismissed. In holding her dismissal to be unfair, the tribunal observed that the fact that the claimant had shown the requisite improvement a year earlier proved that she had it within her ability to improve to an acceptable standard. A reasonable employer would have considered her previous good service and her demonstrated ability to improve, and would have allowed her more time.

In cases of misconduct it may be fair to take into account previous warnings, even if they related to misconduct of a different type to that for which the employee is ultimately dismissed – Auguste Noel Ltd v Curtis 1990 IRLR 326, EAT. However, where a final warning was clearly unreasonable, and where that final warning contributes to a later dismissal, the dismissal may be unfair – Co-operative Retail Services Ltd v Lucas EAT 145/93.

In Polkey v AE Dayton Services Ltd 1988 ICR 142, HL, Lord Bridge observed that in the great majority of cases employers will not be considered to have acted reasonably in dismissing for incapability unless they have given the employee fair warning and a chance to improve. In practice, most employers will have already incorporated a system of warnings into their dismissal procedures. Even before Polkey, warnings were considered a necessary procedural requirement, particularly in cases of misconduct, and this requirement was applied to dismissals for capability as early as 1973 – Winterhalter Gastronom Ltd v Webb 1973 ICR 245, NIRC.

Lapsed warnings. It cannot be assumed that warnings automatically lapse at the end of an improvement period. Whether it can be inferred that the warning has lapsed will depend on the circumstances. This was made clear in Kraft Foods Ltd v Fox 1978 ICR 311, where the EAT said: 'There is sometimes a tendency for a warning to be regarded as having lapsed if a period of time has gone by. In certain circumstances, of course, that may be true. Here, however, the company were dealing with a man who, in the end, was not capable of doing the job; he fell short of the requirements. It seems to us that it is wrong to say that, where a man has been given six months in which to improve, if the employer gives him a further period of time beyond the six months, the employer is to be criticised thereafter for saying that the employee did not act in accordance with the warning at the end of the period of time. It may well be that the employer is being over-generous; but being over-generous is not the same thing as being unreasonable.'

Expired warnings. It will not necessarily be unreasonable for employers to rely on a prior warning that has expired. In Airbus UK Ltd v Webb 2008 ICR 561, CA, the claimant was the only one of four employees caught watching television outside the normal break time to be dismissed. The other three, who were given a final written warning, had no prior disciplinary record, whereas W had previously been given a final written warning which had expired three weeks before. In reaching its decision, the Court of Appeal distinguished a decision of the Court of Session in Diosynth Ltd v Thomson 2006 IRLR 284 where it was held that an employer had acted unreasonably in taking into account an expired warning when deciding to dismiss an employee, commenting that that case was not authority for a broad proposition that an expired warning must be ignored for all purposes.

Consistency of treatment. As the Acas Guide points out, fairness does not mean that similar offences will always call for the same disciplinary action (page 28). Each case must be looked at in the context of its particular circumstances, which may include health or domestic problems, provocation, or justifiable ignorance of the rule or standard involved. The Guide gives two scenarios based on an example involving disciplinary action taken against an employee who has made a series of mistakes concerning delivery dates with the result that a customer has threatened to take its business elsewhere. In the first scenario, the employee had received relevant training and her team leader and section manager had stressed to her the importance of agreeing delivery dates. In the second, she had received no training or guidance from her supervisor or manager. In the first scenario, a final written warning was deemed appropriate, whereas no disciplinary action was warranted in the second.

In Paul v East Surrey District Health Authority 1995 IRLR 305 the Court of Appeal held that an employer is entitled to take into account not only the nature of the conduct and the surrounding facts but also any personal circumstances affecting the employee. That case concerned a nurse who was dismissed for drinking on duty. He argued that his dismissal was unfair since colleagues who had also been drinking on duty had not been dismissed. The Court found that the attitude of the employee to his or her conduct may be a relevant factor in deciding whether a repetition of it is likely and commented: 'Thus an employee who admits that the conduct proved is unacceptable and accepts advice and help to avoid a repetition may be regarded differently from one who refuses to accept responsibility for his actions, argues with management or makes unfounded suggestions that his fellow employees have conspired to accuse him falsely.'

The employer must consider the circumstances of each individual employee. Two contrasting examples:

- **Merseyside Passenger Transport Executive v Millington** EAT 232/89: M worked on a passenger ferry. During one of his shifts he went to a pub to have lunch. He was joined by two other employees, H and W. The employer had a strict rule that employees should not enter licensed premises while working. A member of management went to the pub and immediately suspended all three employees. There was no suggestion that M was drunk – he had merely gone to the most convenient place to obtain food – but H and W acted in a way consistent with their being drunk. On the following day, all three were summarily dismissed. Management believed that it risked an unfair dismissal claim if it did not treat all three alike for breaching the same rule. However, the tribunal took the view that there were enough differences between M's conduct and that of H and W, coupled with mitigating factors on M's behalf, to make a reasonable employer distinguish between them and treat M more leniently. The EAT agreed. It added that to treat all employees the same as a matter of course, without considering the particular circumstances of each individual, simply could not be done

- **Levenes Solicitors v Dalley** 2008 EWCA Civ 69: the Court of Appeal found that the employer had not acted unreasonably in dismissing D for failing to issue a claim in time when another solicitor who had failed to serve proceedings in time on three occasions had not been dismissed. The fact that D was also facing a charge of being absent from work for no good reason justified the difference in treatment.

41

First written warning. Paragraph 18 of the Code states that where misconduct is confirmed or the employee is found to be performing unsatisfactorily it is usual to give the employee a written warning. The employee should also be given sufficient time in which to improve. An example:

- **British Sulphur Corporation v Lawrie** EAT 159/86: a researcher acquitted herself well in most aspects of her job but her written work for the company journal was substandard. She told her departmental head that she did not want to write any more articles and shortly afterwards she was dismissed. The EAT upheld a tribunal decision that she was unfairly dismissed. The company had given her no warning about the consequences of a failure to improve and an insufficient period of time during which any improvement could be assessed. If the employee had been formally warned that failure to improve would mean dismissal she might have agreed to write articles and with instruction might have improved.

Employers may have as many stages in their procedures as they consider appropriate. For example, some procedures may include an 'informal' stage (although note that if such action results in a written record it may not be viewed as informal for the purpose of the right to be accompanied – see Chapter 6) and/or more than one formal warning stage before a final written warning is given. What is important is that parties are aware of which stage has been reached and its consequences.

Paragraph 20 of the Code specifies that a written warning, whether first or final, should set out the nature of the misconduct or poor performance and the change to behaviour or improvement in performance required, with a timescale. The employee should be told how long the warning will remain current and informed of the consequences of further misconduct, or failure to improve performance, within the set period – for instance, in the case of a final warning, that it may result in dismissal or some other contractual penalty such as demotion or loss of seniority. A failure by the employer to comply with any of these requirements may make it unreasonable to rely on the warning in any future disciplinary action.

In cases of poor performance, the Acas Guide recommends that the employee be given an 'improvement note' setting out:

- the performance problem

- the improvement required

- the timescale for achieving this improvement

- a review date, and

- any support, including any training, that the employer will provide to assist the employee (page 28).

The employee should also be informed that the note represents the first stage of a formal procedure equivalent to a first written warning and that failure to improve could lead to a final written warning and, ultimately, dismissal. A copy of the note should be kept and used as the basis for monitoring and reviewing performance over a specified period (e.g. six months).

In the case of misconduct, the Guide suggests that the written warning should set out:

- the nature of the misconduct

- the change in behaviour required (page 29).

It should also inform the employee that a final written warning may be considered if there is further misconduct. A record of the warning should be kept, but it should be disregarded for disciplinary purposes after a specified period (e.g. six months).

The Guide also suggests that the warning should inform the employee of his or her right to appeal and the timescale within which an appeal must be made.

Final written warning. A further act of misconduct or failure to improve performance within a set period would normally result in a final written warning (para 18). However, where an employee's first misconduct or unsatisfactory performance is sufficiently serious – for example, it has had or may have had a serious harmful impact on the organisation – it may be appropriate to move directly to a final written warning (para 19).

A final written warning may also be used where misconduct is sufficiently serious to amount to gross misconduct justifying summary dismissal but the circumstances are such that dismissal is not deemed appropriate, as illustrated by the following example taken from page 30 of the Acas Guide:

> A long-serving employee returns from a celebratory lunch having consumed too much alcohol. He is very apologetic and promises that it will not happen again. Although being unfit for work because of excessive alcohol is listed in the company rules as gross misconduct, taking into account his ten years' service and exemplary record, the employer decides not to dismiss but to give him a final written warning.

Time limits for warnings. There is no set time limit for a written warning: the Code only requires that a timescale be included (para 20) and the example of six months given in the Guide is purely that. The Guide recommends that, 'except in agreed special circumstances, any disciplinary action taken should be disregarded for disciplinary purposes after a specified period of satisfactory conduct or performance' (page 33). It states that normal practice is for different types of warnings to remain in force for different periods; for example, six months for a first written warning and 12 months for a final written warning (or more in exceptional circumstances). It suggests that the established period should be set out in the disciplinary procedure and that warnings should cease to be 'live' when that period has expired. However, the Guide does provide for exceptions. First, where there is a pattern of an employee's conduct improving during the period of a warning and lapsing shortly afterwards, the Guide suggests that his or her previous record can be taken into account when deciding how long a future warning should last. Secondly, although stating that a decision to dismiss should not be based on an expired warning, the Guide accepts that the fact that there is an expired warning may explain an employer's decision not to substitute a lesser penalty.

Since an employee's prior disciplinary record is often a factor in deciding whether dismissal is an appropriate sanction, both parties will benefit from knowing whether a previous warning has expired.

Dismissal. Paragraph 21 of the Code makes it clear that a decision to dismiss should only be taken by a manager who has the authority to do so and that the employee should be informed as soon as possible of the reasons for the dismissal, the date on which the employment contract will end, the appropriate period of notice and the right of appeal.

An employee with at least a year's service at the effective date of termination has a statutory right under S.92 ERA to receive a written statement of the reasons for his or her dismissal if he or she requests one. If such a request is made, the employer must provide the statement within 14 days. An employee who is pregnant or who is on maternity or adoption leave which is brought to an end by the dismissal is entitled to written reasons for dismissal without having to make a request and regardless of length of service. A failure to provide written reasons will result in an award of two weeks' pay to the employee – S.93 ERA (see IDS Employment Law Handbook, 'Unfair Dismissal' (2005), Chapter 20).

Other sanctions. If the disciplinary rules provide for sanctions other than dismissal, such as transfer, demotion or suspension without pay, the employer should consider whether such an alternative is appropriate – see page 30 of the Acas Guide.

The question of alternative employment is normally considered relevant to an employer's reasonableness in dismissing where there has been little or no contributory behaviour on the part of the employee dismissed – for example, in situations of incapacity and redundancy. However, P v Nottinghamshire County Council 1992 ICR 706, CA, appears to have extended this duty to consider redeployment into certain misconduct cases. In that case P was dismissed from his position as an assistant groundsman at a girls' school run by Nottinghamshire County Council. He had pleaded guilty to a charge of indecent assault against his daughter and asked for two further offences of indecent conduct with two older daughters to be taken into account. At the time of his dismissal he was informed that an attempt would be made by the Council to redeploy him in the Highways Department. However, he was not accepted there on account of his sickness record. His complaint of unfair dismissal was upheld by a tribunal in a majority decision. On appeal, the Court of Appeal stated that in an appropriate case, and where the size and administrative resources of the employer's undertaking permit, it may be unfair to dismiss an employee without first considering whether he or she could be redeployed in an alternative job, notwithstanding that it is clear that the employee could not be allowed to continue in his or her original job. Unfortunately, the judgment gives no real guidance as to what might constitute an 'appropriate case' when it comes to dismissals for misconduct. It may well be that in misconduct cases alternative employment should only be investigated where the dismissal would not have been regarded as necessary in the first place if the employee had been employed in a different post.

Provide employees with an opportunity to appeal

Paragraph 25 of the Code states that: 'Where an employee feels that disciplinary action taken against them is wrong or unjust they should appeal against the decision. Appeals should be heard without unreasonable delay and ideally at an agreed time and place. Employees should let employers know the grounds for their appeal in writing.' This makes it clear that the right to appeal applies to *all* disciplinary hearings, not just those resulting in dismissal, with the result that a refusal to allow an employee to appeal at *any* stage of the procedure could lead to an uplift in any compensation award if the employee subsequently brings a successful tribunal claim. It also imposes an obligation on the employee to appeal in writing, with the result that any failure to do so may be taken into account by an employment tribunal when determining any related claim and any resulting compensation may be reduced accordingly under S.207A TULR(C)A – see Chapter 5 under 'Adjustment to tribunal awards'. Delay by either party also has the potential to incur a penalty.

The Guide states that the opportunity to appeal against a disciplinary decision is essential to natural justice and that an appeal may be raised on any number of grounds such as new evidence, undue severity or inconsistency of the penalty (page 33). It also says that an appeal can be either a review of the disciplinary sanction or a rehearing, which reflects the Court of Appeal's judgment in Taylor v OCS Group Ltd 2006 ICR 1602. In that case the Court held that the task for a tribunal when considering whether the employer acted reasonably in dismissing is to assess the fairness of the disciplinary process as a whole. Where procedural deficiencies occur at an early stage, the tribunal should examine the subsequent appeal hearing, particularly its procedural fairness and thoroughness, and the open-mindedness of the decision-maker.

The Guide warns against using an appeal to punish the employee for appealing and recommends that it should not result in any increase in the penalty as this may deter individuals from appealing (page 34). The employee has a statutory right to be accompanied at an appeal hearing (see Chapter 6).

The Code states that: 'The appeal should be dealt with impartially and, wherever possible, by a manager who has not previously been involved in the case' (para 26). Unless there is no alternative, an appeal heard by someone who has already been involved in the disciplinary proceedings is likely to make a dismissal unfair. For example:

- **Byrne v BOC Ltd** 1992 IRLR 505, EAT: B was suspected of falsifying her overtime claims and the matter was investigated by assistant manager P1 and manager P2. Both consulted the employee relations manager, who advised them that such action warranted instant dismissal. B was subsequently dismissed by P1 at a hastily arranged disciplinary hearing, instigated by P2. B's appeal was heard by P2. A tribunal found that although the initial dismissal was unfair because B had not been given sufficient warning of the charges against her, the defects had been cured by the appeal, rendering the dismissal fair. The EAT disagreed, finding that P2's involvement in the early stages of the disciplinary process made him a 'judge in his own cause' and consequently incapable of putting right the earlier defects. In so holding, the EAT confirmed that involvement in the investigation can disqualify a person from hearing the appeal as much as his or her personal involvement in the events that led to dismissal.

However, in very small organisations, or where there is a limited hierarchy, there may be no other person who can hear an appeal and in these circumstances a departure from the Code is likely to be seen as reasonable. For example, in Royal Naval School v Hughes 1979 IRLR 383 the EAT, while upholding a finding of unfair dismissal, commented that the absence of any appeal structure beyond the board of governors of the school to resolve grievances was not in itself unfair.

Employees should be informed in writing of the results of the appeal hearing 'as soon as possible' (para 28).

Special cases
There are certain situations in which special considerations apply. These are where the employee is a trade union representative, has been charged or convicted of a criminal offence, or is a probationer.

Trade union representatives. The Code recommends that: 'Where disciplinary action is being considered against an employee who is a trade union representative the normal disciplinary procedure should be followed. Depending on the circumstances, however, it is advisable to discuss the matter at an early stage with an official employed by the union, after obtaining the employee's agreement.' The Guide explains that this is because 'disciplinary action against a trade union representative can be construed as an attack on the union if not handled carefully' (page 35). Any disciplinary action that is instituted *because* an individual is a trade union representative (or member) will constitute an unlawful detriment contrary to S.146 TULR(C)A, and dismissal for that reason will be automatically unfair by virtue of S.152 TULR(C)A.

Criminal charge or conviction. Where an employee has been charged with, or convicted of, a criminal offence, it does not necessarily follow that disciplinary action is justified. The Acas Code recommends that employers consider the effect of the charge or conviction on the employee's suitability to do the job and his or her relationship with the employer, colleagues and customers (para 30).

Where criminal proceedings are pending, matters can become complicated. For example, internal enquiries will often be hampered by the employee's reluctance to discuss the incident. Nevertheless, the employer should do his best to satisfy himself of the employee's guilt before taking disciplinary action. If the employer can show that he believes, after carrying out a reasonable investigation, that the employee is guilty of misconduct meriting dismissal, then a subsequent acquittal on a criminal charge arising out of the same events will not of itself make dismissal unfair. In Ali v Sovereign Buses (London) Ltd 0274/06 the EAT reviewed the authorities on the issue and concluded that there is no hard-and-fast rule as to what an employer should do when deciding whether to press ahead with disciplinary proceedings when there is a criminal trial pending. It will depend on the circumstances of the case, although the employer should not dismiss too easily.

Probationers. Employees on probation are a special case because tribunals and courts consider it particularly important that reasonable steps be taken to maintain appraisal of probationers throughout the probationary period. This was stressed by the EAT in Post Office v Mughal 1977 ICR 763, where it said that: 'The question for the... tribunal is: have the employers shown that they took reasonable steps to maintain appraisal of the probationer throughout the period of probation, giving guidance by advice or warning when such was likely to be useful or fair; and that an appropriate officer made an honest effort to determine whether the probationer came up to the required standard, having informed himself of the appraisals made by supervising officers and any other facts recorded about the probationer? If this procedure is followed, it is only if the officer responsible for deciding upon selection of probationers then arrives at a decision which no reasonable assessment could dictate, that [a] tribunal should hold the dismissal to be unfair.'

Insufficient appraisal and training rendered the dismissal of a probationer unfair in Herity v Ashbury Confectionery Ltd ET Case No.1902731/03. In that case the claimant began working for the employer as a machine operator on 15 April 2002 on a three-month probationary period. Two weeks after beginning work he was involved in a road traffic accident and was off work for six months, in view of which his probationary period was extended. On 30 September 2003, during the currency of the extended probationary period, the claimant was summarily dismissed for lack of capability. The tribunal held his dismissal to be unfair. The employer had failed to provide adequate training and, as a probationer, the claimant was in a special category of employee in respect of whom it was especially important to carry out regular appraisals. The lack of appraisal and proper training was probably enough to make the dismissal unfair; but coupled with the way that the dismissal was carried out, with little or no formal procedure, the decision to dismiss certainly fell outside the band of reasonable responses.

In White v London Transport Executive 1981 IRLR 261, EAT, it was argued, on the basis of the principle laid down in Mughal, that there is an implied term in every probationary contract of employment that the employer is bound to support, assist, offer guidance to and train the probationary employee. The EAT rejected this argument, but said that 'the right term to imply is… an obligation on the employer to take reasonable steps to maintain an appraisal of a probationer during a trial period, giving guidance by advice or warning where necessary'. A failure to guide and train may render an otherwise fair dismissal unfair – ILEA v Lloyd 1981 IRLR 394, CA.

Sickness absence

As mentioned at the beginning of this chapter, it is not entirely clear whether the Code applies to sickness absence situations. While the Code does not specifically refer to sickness absence, it does not rule it out either. Moreover, the accompanying Guide devotes a considerable amount of space to the issue (see Appendix 4: 'Dealing with absence'). Since sickness absence can lead to dismissal, the fairness of which falls to be determined under S.98(4) ERA, an employer will need to establish that he followed a fair procedure in deciding that dismissal was reasonable in the circumstances. As we discuss below, a fair procedure will contain elements that are covered by the Code of Practice, such as establishing the facts, and arguably tribunals will be entitled to take the Code into account when deciding whether a dismissal is fair, and to apply the adjustment provisions of S.207A TULR(C)A where it has not been complied with (see Chapter 5 under 'Adjustment to tribunal awards'). On the other hand, the Acas Guide recommends that an employee who is dismissed on ill-health grounds is 'informed of any right to appeal'. This suggests that it does not view a right of appeal as an *essential* requirement, which in turn suggests that the Code does not in fact apply. And there is at least one EAT decision that states that genuine illness should not be treated as a disciplinary matter (Lynock v Cereal Packaging Ltd 1988 ICR 670), which adds weight to this view. Conversely, the Guide suggests that short-term absences may, at least in some circumstances, be dealt with as a disciplinary matter, in which case the Code

48

would apply. Both long-term absence, as in the case of a serious illness or injury, and frequent short absences over a long period of time may constitute grounds for dismissal, but procedures differ depending on which category the absence falls into.

In practice, application of the Code may depend on whether an employee's absence is viewed as justified – in which case it will be a capability issue and the Code will not apply – or not, in which case it will be a conduct matter and employers should follow the Code as discussed under 'Conduct and capability' above. However, this can be a dangerous distinction to make – as the case law set out below demonstrates – and employers should carry out the necessary investigations, including obtaining medical evidence where appropriate, before any action is taken. Since the purpose of an investigation is to establish the facts, this is the equivalent of the first step recommended in the Acas Code. A properly conducted investigation should then establish the next appropriate step to be taken. Below, we set out the procedural steps that have been found to apply in cases of long-term and short-term sickness absence. First, however, we consider a number of miscellaneous issues that should be borne in mind when dealing with sickness absences.

Disability discrimination. It is important to note that if an employee's absence is the result of an underlying illness which amounts to a disability under the Disability Discrimination Act 1995 special considerations apply, as a dismissal may amount to unlawful discrimination even if it is found to be fair under the ERA. In particular, an employer has a duty to make reasonable adjustments in relation to a disabled employee, so he will need to consider whether additional steps are necessary in the disciplinary procedure. Disability discrimination is discussed further in IDS Employment Law Handbook, 'Disability Discrimination' (2002).

Data Protection. When dealing with employees' health records, employers should pay heed to the Data Protection Act 1998, as medical information will constitute 'sensitive personal data' under that Act. The Information Commissioner has issued a Data Protection Code covering this area, the 'Employment Practices Data Protection Code Part 4: Information about Workers' Health', together with supplementary guidance, to which employers should refer (see www.ico.gov.uk).

Medical reports. The Access to Medical Reports Act 1988 gives individuals certain rights in respect of reports relating to their health that have been prepared by a medical practitioner 'who is or has been responsible for the clinical care of the individual'. Under that Act:

- an employer who wishes to contact an employee's doctor must notify the employee in writing and must have his or her written consent before doing so

49

- in giving such notification the employer must inform the individual of his or her right to withhold consent; to have access to the report and to then withhold consent for it to be supplied; and to request amendments to the report

- if the employee states that he or she wishes to have access to the report the employer must tell the doctor when making the application and at the same time let the employee know that the report has been requested

- the employee must contact the doctor within 21 days of the date of the application to make arrangements to see the report

- if the employee considers the report to be incorrect or misleading he or she can make a written request to have it amended

- if the doctor refuses to amend the report, the employee has the right to ask him or her to attach a statement to it reflecting the employee's view on any matters of disagreement

- the employee has the right to withhold consent for the report to be supplied to the employer.

Note that the 1988 Act only covers reports prepared by a medical practitioner responsible for the worker's care. If a report is requested by an occupational health consultant instructed by the employer, for example, the individual's rights to access will be limited to those provided by the Data Protection Act 1998 (see above).

Long-term sickness absence

Case law shows that the fairness of a dismissal on the ground of long-term ill health will depend on:

- consultation with the employee

- medical investigation, and

- consideration, where appropriate, of alternative employment.

Consultation. In the context of sickness absence, consultation has two purposes: to balance the employer's need for the work to be done against the employee's need for time to recover; and to ensure that steps are taken to establish the true medical position – Taylorplan Catering (Scotland) Ltd v McInally 1980 IRLR 53, EAT. Often employers will need to obtain medical opinion (with the employee's consent).

The EAT stressed the importance of consultation and discovering the true medical position in the leading case of East Lindsey District Council v Daubney 1977 ICR 566, where Mr Justice Phillips said: 'Unless there are wholly exceptional circumstances, before an employee is dismissed on the ground of ill health it is necessary that he should be consulted and the matter discussed with

50

him, and that in one way or another steps should be taken by the employer to discover the true medical position. We do not propose to lay down detailed principles to be applied in such cases, for what will be necessary in one case may not be appropriate in another. But if in every case employers take such steps as are sensible according to the circumstances to consult the employee and to discuss the matter with him, and to inform themselves upon the true medical position, it will be found in practice that all that is necessary has been done. Discussions and consultation will often bring to light facts and circumstances of which the employers were unaware, and which will throw new light on the problem. Or the employee may wish to seek medical advice on his own account, which, brought to the notice of the employers' medical advisers, will cause them to change their opinion. There are many possibilities. Only one thing is certain, and that is that if the employee is not consulted, and given an opportunity to state his case, an injustice may be done.'

There have been a number of cases where a failure to consult the employee has resulted in a finding of unfair dismissal. The following is a good example:

- **East Lindsey District Council v Daubney** 1977 ICR 566, EAT: D was dismissed on the ground of ill health. The Council had acted upon a report prepared by its physician. The physician had based his report on an examination carried out by another doctor. The dismissal was found unfair because D had not had an opportunity to state his case or to obtain an independent medical opinion. Furthermore, the Council had not obtained a full medical report before deciding to dismiss.

The Acas Guide recommends that where an employee is on long-term sick leave, the employee and employer keep in regular contact with each other and that the employee be kept fully informed if there is any risk to employment. Even if an employer has obtained medical evidence, it is important to consult the employee before a decision to dismiss is taken, since the medical report may have been misconstrued – WM Computer Services Ltd v Passmore EAT 721/86.

Medical investigation. In the Daubney case, above, the EAT commented that it is not the function of employers to set themselves up as medical experts. Rather, the question they have to ask is an employment one – whether to dismiss in the light of available medical advice.

A failure to seek proper medical advice (where this is appropriate) is likely to result in a finding of unfair dismissal. For example:

- **Parsons and Co Ltd v Kidney** EAT 788/87: after K had been absent for several weeks her doctor informed the employer that she was suffering either from back strain or from a slipped disc. Recovery from the former would take about six weeks, and from the latter about 12. The employer arbitrarily chose to accept the more serious of the two diagnoses and dismissed K instead of attempting to clarify the complaint. The EAT found the dismissal unfair. Not only had there been a failure to consult with K, there had also been a failure to establish clearly the nature of her disability and the likely length of her absence.

The first medical opinion sought should normally be that of the employee's own GP. However, a request for such information must be made in accordance with the requirements of the Access to Medical Reports Act 1988 as set out above (see 'Medical reports'), which includes first obtaining the employee's consent. If consent is received, the GP should be asked the nature of the illness, the expected period of absence and what type of work the employee will be capable of on his or her return to work. A dismissal may well be held to be unfair if an employer simply relies on the opinion of a third party such as a company doctor – see East Lindsey District Council v Daubney (above).

Where there is doubt as to the nature of the illness or injury, the employer may ask the employee to consult a specialist or agree to be examined by a doctor to be appointed by the organisation. For example:

- **Crampton v Dacorum Motors Ltd** 1975 IRLR 168, ET: C, a service manager, was diagnosed by his GP as suffering from angina and advised to rest for four weeks. The company made informal enquiries about the nature of this condition and decided to dismiss. A tribunal held that the employer had acted unreasonably in dismissing a man over 50 from a position of responsibility on the basis of a GP's diagnosis. The employer should have invited the employee to submit to a further examination by a specialist, 'preferably, but not necessarily, selected by the employer'.

If there is conflicting medical evidence, the employer is entitled to rely on one opinion in favour of the other as long as he has good reason for doing so. For example, in Heathrow Express Operating Co Ltd v Jenkins EAT 0497/06 the employer was entitled to rely on the opinion of an occupational health specialist who had knowledge of the working environment over that of a consultant psychiatrist.

If the employee refuses to cooperate in providing medical evidence, or to undergo an independent medical examination, the Acas Guide recommends that he or she be told in writing that a decision will be taken on the basis of the information available and that it could result in dismissal. Dismissal in those circumstances may be fair:

- **McIntosh v John Brown Engineering** Ltd EAT 339/90: M was a site engineer working overseas. After five years he had a nervous breakdown and was treated for anxiety. He was examined by the company doctor and returned to work but several complaints were received about his behaviour. Legislation was brought out requiring overseas staff to be medically fit. M refused to be examined by the company doctor and refused to allow the company to keep a report prepared by his own doctor. He also refused to be examined by an independent medical specialist and was dismissed. The EAT, upholding the tribunal's finding of fair dismissal, felt that in the face of M's recalcitrance the employer was entitled to feel that there was no option but to dismiss.

Alternative employment. A failure on an employer's part to consider alternative employment for an employee suffering from ill health may be sufficient to render a dismissal unfair. For example:

- **Dick v Boots the Chemist Ltd** EAT 68/91: D, a store detective, was severely assaulted by a shoplifter she had apprehended. She was absent from work 'indefinitely'. Almost three years later a doctor reported that it was unlikely that she would ever be fit for her job again. The tribunal was satisfied that there had been sufficient consultation – with the employee, her medical advisers and the company's welfare services manager – and was prepared to excuse the employer's failure to consider alternative employment on the ground that, on the basis of the doctor's report, this would have been futile. The EAT disagreed and said the tribunal had erred. The company's procedure had been seriously flawed by the complete failure to consider the question of alternative employment.

An employer does not have to create a special job where none exists – Merseyside and North Wales Electricity Board v Taylor 1975 ICR 185, QBD. However, he should consider a wide range of jobs even if there might not be an obvious match:

- **Silver v Royal Borough of Windsor and Maidenhead** ET Case No.2536/88: S had limited vision in her left eye and light/dark perception only in her right eye. Her vision and performance deteriorated during her 20 years of employment. Despite a full medical investigation and a proper decision being taken that she could no longer carry on in her job, a tribunal found her dismissal unfair. The employer had failed to offer her alternative employment as a telephonist/receptionist on either a permanent or a trial basis. This was not excused by the employer's belief that S had an unsuitable temperament for such work.

An employer may need to consider offering training to an employee so that he or she can take up an alternative job – Smith v Network Rail Infrastructure Ltd EAT 0047/07.

Where the ill health arises because of the nature of the work itself, employers may not be acting reasonably if they fail to take reasonable steps to remove the cause. So, for example, in Jagdeo v Smiths Industries Ltd 1982 ICR 47 J became ill when moved to a new factory department that required her to do more soldering than before. She became allergic to solder fumes. Unsuccessful attempts were made to alleviate the problem by the use of three different types of mask. No alternative work was available for her. However, an officer of the

Health and Safety Executive had suggested that the problem had been successfully eliminated at other factories by the use of an extractor fan. The EAT held that in the absence of any explanation from the company as to what steps, if any, had been taken regarding the use of an extractor fan, it was impossible for the tribunal to decide whether the employer had acted reasonably. The case was remitted to be heard on that point. And in Thanet District Council v Websper EAT 1090/01 the EAT upheld a tribunal's decision that, in refusing to transfer an employee to an alternative role to alleviate work stress, the Council had breached an implied term that it should provide a safe place to work, leading to a finding of unfair constructive dismissal.

Note that if the employee is entitled to an ill-health pension the employer must consider ill-health retirement before dismissing on the ground of incapacity – First West Yorkshire Ltd t/a First Leeds v Haigh 2008 IRLR 182, EAT.

Alcohol or drug dependency. The Acas Guide suggests that consideration should be given to introducing measures to help employees who are suffering from alcohol or drug abuse, or from stress. The aim should be to identify employees affected and encourage them to seek help and treatment. Sample policies for managing alcohol and drug problems can be found in the Acas advisory booklet, 'Health, work and wellbeing', available on the Acas website (www.acas.org.uk).

Needless to say, an employer should follow the in-house policy if there is one. In Sinclair v Wandsworth Council EAT 0145/07 the EAT held that the Council's failure to implement its alcohol policy when disciplining an employee made the dismissal unfair.

Persistent short-term absences

The Guide makes the following recommendations in relation to handling persistent short-term absences:

- unexpected absences should be investigated promptly and the employee asked for an explanation at a return-to-work interview

- if there are no acceptable reasons then the employer may wish to treat the matter as a conduct issue and deal with it under the disciplinary procedure

- where there is no medical certificate to support frequent short-term, self-certified absences, then the employee should be asked to see a doctor to establish whether treatment is necessary and whether the underlying reason for the absence is work-related. If no medical support is forthcoming, the employer should consider whether to take action under the disciplinary procedure

- in all cases the employee should be told what improvement in attendance is expected and warned of the likely consequences if this does not happen

- if there is no improvement, the employee's length of service, performance, the likelihood of a change in attendance, the availability of suitable alternative work where appropriate and the effect of past and future absences on the organisation should all be taken into account in deciding appropriate action.

It also advises employers to keep absence records so that absence can be monitored and any problems addressed at an early stage, and to deal with persistent absence promptly, firmly and consistently in order to show both the employee concerned and other employees that absence is regarded as a serious matter. However, employers should avoid making decisions that are primarily intended to communicate a message to the rest of the workforce: in Leeson v Makita Manufacturing Europe Ltd EAT 0911/00 the EAT found a dismissal unfair when it had more to do with the employer's wish to make an example of the employee to deter others than with dealing with his genuine sickness absence.

In some cases of short-term absence a formal medical investigation may not prove fruitful because of the transient nature of the employee's symptoms and complaints. In such cases there comes a time when a reasonable employer is entitled to say 'enough is enough' and, so long as warnings have been given, he will be justified in treating the frequent absences as a sufficient reason for dismissing. In Rolls-Royce Ltd v Walpole 1980 IRLR 343, EAT, for example, W's absenteeism record averaged about 50 per cent for the last three years of his employment. The employer, finding no pattern in his absences, gave him warnings that the absences were getting out of hand and followed company procedure meticulously. Since there seemed no reason to anticipate any improvement, W was eventually dismissed. The EAT allowed the employer's appeal against a tribunal's finding that the dismissal was unfair, stressing that, for a dismissal to be fair, all that needs to be shown is that the decision to dismiss was within the range of responses which a reasonable employer could have made.

It is important that an employer does not make assumptions about an employee's absences and gives him or her an opportunity to explain. As the cases below show, treating genuine sickness absence as misconduct can lead to a finding of unfair dismissal.

In International Sports Co Ltd v Thomson 1980 IRLR 340 the EAT stated that what is required where there is an unacceptable level of intermittent absence is:

- a fair review by the employer of the attendance record and the reasons for absence

- an opportunity for the employee to make representations

- appropriate warnings of dismissal if things do not improve.

If there is no adequate improvement in the attendance record, then, said the EAT, dismissal will be justifiable. This is likely to be so regardless of the employee's length of service – see, for example, Regan v Magnetti Marelli UK Ltd EAT 577/99.

Fair review and opportunity to make representations. Reviewing the employee's record and giving the employee an opportunity to make representations may bring to light an underlying medical condition. If it does, it is suggested that the employer seek proper medical advice in order to determine the extent and likely duration of the medical condition, and whether, and if so how soon, treatment will bring the absenteeism down to an acceptable level. Particular consideration should be given to the question of whether the underlying condition amounts to a disability under the Disability Discrimination Act 1995. If it does, the employer should consider whether there are any reasonable adjustments that could be made to help the employee. The employer should also be aware that any dismissal might amount to disability discrimination.

If it is clear that the nature of the underlying condition is such that there is unlikely to be any improvement, then the case should be regarded as one of long-term illness and the appropriate steps taken. Two illustrations:

- **Smith v Van Den Berghs and Jurgens Ltd** ET Case No.11351/79: the employer argued that S had been dismissed on account of his 'absenteeism', which was classed as 'misconduct' and not sickness, even though all S's absences were apparently because of genuine illness. The tribunal heard that all the disciplinary procedures had been followed before S was dismissed, including written warnings and suspension, but it nevertheless held the dismissal to be unfair. The tribunal said that such action had been an inappropriate method of dealing with the situation since there was not a 'shred of evidence' that any of the absences was not genuine, and so to call those absences 'misconduct' was a 'misconception and unreasonable'. The majority of S's absences were related to recurrent trouble with an abscess and its treatment, about which no medical evidence had been sought. The tribunal made it clear that its decision might well have been different in this case if the employer had mustered the evidence on the basis of an investigation into S's medical position, instead of treating the case as one of misconduct

- **Devonshire v Trico-Folberth Ltd** 1989 ICR 747, CA: D had had a number of sickness-related absences from work. After several warnings she was dismissed for her 'unacceptable attendance record'. An internal appeal panel decided, on compassionate grounds, that her employment ought to be terminated, not for poor attendance, but because she was medically unfit to do the job. A tribunal said that, had D been dismissed for the original reason – poor attendance – the dismissal would have been fair, but once the ground had been changed to medical unfitness 'the whole picture changed'. It held that the dismissal was unfair because the employer had carried out insufficient investigation into D's medical condition and insufficient consultation with the employee and her GP to warrant dismissal for ill health. The EAT and the Court of Appeal affirmed the tribunal's decision.

However, the Court of Appeal did not impose on employers an absolute obligation to consult the employee's GP in all cases of persistent absenteeism on account of ill health. The proper test in cases of intermittent absenteeism remains that laid down in International Sports (above), and whether medical consultation is necessary depends on the circumstances of each case. In Davis v Tibbett and Britten Group plc EAT 460/99 the employee had a record of persistent short-term absences that were all based on genuine though unconnected medical reasons. In dismissing the employee's appeal against a tribunal's finding that he had not been unfairly dismissed, the EAT cited comments made in the International Sports case to the effect that 'in such a case, it would be placing too heavy a burden on an employer to require him to carry out a formal medical investigation and, even if he did, such an investigation would rarely be fruitful because of the transient nature of the employee's symptoms and complaints'. The EAT added that 'this is not a case where it would be helpful to seek medical evidence'.

Warnings. Although 'warnings' or 'cautions' may seem inappropriate in cases of absence due to illness, they are a necessary measure of fairness for the employee given that such absences may lead to the loss of a job. Formal warnings were certainly viewed as elements going to the reasonableness, and hence fairness, of the dismissals in the International Sports and Rolls-Royce cases (above). In Lynock v Cereal Packaging Ltd 1988 ICR 670 the EAT emphasised that where there was genuine illness it should not be treated as a disciplinary matter and that employers had to treat each case individually with sympathy, understanding and compassion. However, it said the purpose of a 'warnings' system was to give a 'caution' that the stage had been reached where, with the best will in the world, continued employment would become impossible. In practice, employers may find it useful to set absence levels so that if an employee's absence exceeds a certain level, a warnings system will be automatically triggered, bringing the matter to management's attention.

Redundancy

As previously mentioned, the Acas Code specifically states that it does not apply to redundancy dismissals – see the Foreword and para 1. This means that a failure to follow the Code will not result in an uplift in compensation. However, the exclusion of redundancy dismissals from the Code's scope does not mean that employers can dispense with procedural fairness when making redundancies. Redundancy dismissals are covered by the statutory unfair dismissal regime of S.98 ERA in the same way as other dismissals, and in determining whether a dismissal was fair tribunals will have to consider whether it was reasonable in all the circumstances, which includes the overall fairness of the procedure adopted. With the repeal of S.98A ERA and the statutory disciplinary and dismissal procedures (DDPs), gone is the employer's defence that a failure to follow a fair procedure other than the relevant statutory DDP would have made no difference to the decision to dismiss, rendering the dismissal fair. This is discussed in Chapter 5.

In deciding the fairness of redundancy dismissals, tribunals must now rely primarily on case law that was decided before the statutory procedures were introduced in 2004. The leading case is Polkey v AE Dayton Services Ltd 1988 ICR 142, in which the House of Lords established that procedural fairness is an integral part of the reasonableness test in S.98(4) ERA. In the words of Lord Bridge, 'the employer will not normally act reasonably unless he warns and consults any employees affected or their representative, adopts a fair basis on which to select for redundancy and takes such steps as may be reasonable to avoid or minimise the redundancy by deployment within his own organisation'. Thus the core elements of procedural fairness in redundancy cases are:

- consultation

- fair selection, and

- alternative employment.

In Taskforce (Finishing and Handling) Ltd v Love EAT 0001/05 the EAT held that redundancy is not a matter of discipline and there is no right to be accompanied at a redundancy meeting or to appeal against the decision to dismiss. Note, however, that the Acas Advisory booklet, 'Redundancy handling', advises employers to consider the establishment of a redundancy appeals procedure to deal with complaints from employees who feel that selection criteria have been unfairly applied in their case. The booklet, which has been revised in light of the repeal of the statutory procedures, is available on the Acas website (www.acas.org.uk/redundancy).

Below, we examine briefly the three elements of a fair redundancy procedure highlighted in Polkey. For a more detailed analysis of redundancy law and procedures, see IDS Employment Law Handbook, 'Redundancy' (2008).

Consultation

As their Lordships made clear in Polkey, the employer's obligation to consult employees as part of a fair redundancy procedure goes to the question of reasonableness under S.98(4) ERA. In that case, P was dismissed for redundancy without his employer having made any attempt to consult him. The tribunal condemned the company's breach of procedural fairness but decided that P had not been unfairly dismissed because he would have been dismissed even if the company had consulted him. The EAT and the Court of Appeal rejected P's appeal but the House of Lords held that he had been unfairly dismissed. The tribunal should have asked whether the employer had acted reasonably in deciding that the reason for dismissing P was sufficient, not whether P would have been dismissed even if warning or consultation had taken place. Only if the employer could reasonably have concluded at the time of dismissal that the decision to dismiss would be unaffected by any consultation with P could a dismissal in breach of procedural fairness be reasonable.

The subject of the consultation will depend to some extent on the circumstances, but best practice suggests that it should normally include:

- an indication (i.e. warning) that the individual has been provisionally selected for redundancy

- confirmation of the basis for selection

- an opportunity for the employee to comment on his or her redundancy selection assessment

- consideration as to what, if any, alternative positions of employment may exist

- an opportunity for the employee to address any other matters he or she may have.

While the nature of the consultation will inevitably depend on the type of organisation and its size and resources, limited size and resources do not allow an organisation to dispense with consultation altogether. In De Grasse v Stockwell Tools Ltd 1992 IRLR 269 a small firm dismissed a machinist for redundancy with no warning, consultation or consideration of alternative employment. The EAT held that the fact that an employer is a small undertaking may affect the nature or formality of the consultation process – i.e. it may be informal – but it cannot excuse a total lack of consultation.

Case law indicates that consultation is likely to be inadequate if an employee is left in the dark until too late a stage in the redundancy process. The Acas advisory booklet, 'Redundancy handling', states that it is good practice for employers to consult at an early enough stage to allow discussion as to whether the proposed redundancies are necessary at all. Further, the consultation process should precede any public announcement of the redundancy programme and the issue of termination.

It is important to note that the scope of the duty to warn and consult extends only to those employees who are the target of the proposed redundancy. An employer will not be penalised for failing to consult an employee at an earlier stage if the employee was not at risk of redundancy at that time but only became so as a result of subsequent knock-on effects of the original redundancies. To impose such a duty would place much broader obligations on an employer to consider the potential economic consequences of redundancy

59

than are required under the reasonableness test in S.98(4) ERA – Byrne v Arvin Meritor LVS (UK) Ltd EAT 239/02.

Collective redundancies. The employer's duty to consult in respect of collective redundancies is contained in S.188(1) TULR(C)A, which states that 'where an employer is proposing to dismiss as redundant 20 or more employees at one establishment within a period of 90 days or less, the employer shall consult about the dismissals all the persons who are appropriate representatives of any of the employees who may be affected by measures taken in connection with those dismissals'. S.188 goes on to set out details of when and how that consultation should be carried out. A failure to comply with S.188 may lead to a tribunal making a collective award under S.189.

For a detailed examination of the collective consultation requirements, see IDS Employment Law Handbook, 'Redundancy' (2008), Chapter 11.

Fair selection

If an employer adopts unfair selection criteria, or applies them in a subjective or otherwise unreasonable way, this will amount to a breach of the procedural requirements and is likely to make the dismissal procedurally unfair under Polkey. Furthermore, such action will undermine the basic premise that redundancy is the true reason for dismissal, thereby rendering the dismissal potentially substantively unfair. If a tribunal finds that the real reason for dismissal was not redundancy but some other reason, it is arguable that it can adjust any compensation awarded under S.207A TULR(C)A on the ground that the employer unreasonably failed to comply with the Code (see Chapter 5 under 'Adjustment to tribunal awards'). An uplift may also be applied where, although the dismissal was for redundancy, the selection for redundancy was for a reason that *is* covered by the Code, e.g. a discriminatory reason such as race or sex.

One principle that was established by case law decided under the statutory DDPs was that employees facing redundancy were entitled to be informed of the selection criteria being used and their individual score against those criteria so that they had a chance to challenge them at the dismissal meeting – see Alexander and anor v Bridgen Enterprises Ltd 2006 ICR 1277, EAT, where the employer's failure to provide this information meant that Step 2 of the DDP had not been observed and the redundancy dismissals were therefore automatically unfair.

Although such a failure would no longer make a dismissal *automatically* unfair (as the DDPs have been repealed), it would nevertheless be open to a tribunal to find that a failure to provide reasons for selection and an opportunity to challenge them could give rise to a breach of the ordinary principles of fairness in a redundancy procedure. Indeed, such a finding must be thought likely. However, there is the possibility that such a breach could be 'cured' at a later stage in the procedure; for example, at a later meeting or on appeal – see Lloyd v Taylor Woodrow Construction 1999 IRLR 782, EAT.

Alternative employment

The consideration of alternative employment for employees selected for redundancy will often be an important part of a fair and reasonable redundancy procedure. Although this is not a statutory requirement (except where the employee is on maternity leave – see Chapter 5), Lord Bridge established in Polkey that the potential for the redeployment of redundant employees within the organisation is something that a reasonable employer will consider and an employer should do what he can so far as is reasonable to seek alternative work for an employee facing redundancy. This does not mean that he is obliged by law to enquire about job opportunities elsewhere, and a failure to do so will not necessarily render a dismissal unfair. However, as a general rule, tribunals will expect an employer with sufficient resources to take reasonable steps to alleviate the effects of redundancy, including giving detailed consideration to whether suitable alternative employment is available.

In Fisher v Hoopoe Finance Ltd EAT 0043/05, the EAT suggested that an employer's responsibility does not necessarily end with drawing the employee's attention to job vacancies that may be suitable. The employer should also provide information about the financial implications of taking up any vacant alternative positions. A failure to do so may lead to any later redundancy dismissal being found to be unfair.

Redundancy payments

An examination of the law governing redundancy payments falls outside the scope of this Supplement. However, one rather curious anomaly which we should mention here is that, while the Acas Code does not apply to redundancy dismissals, it *does* apply to redundancy payment claims (see Schedule A2 to the TULR(C)A, reproduced in Appendix 1 to this Supplement). This means that if an employer unreasonably fails to comply with the Code when determining an employee's entitlement to a redundancy payment, the compensation adjustment provisions will apply. For further details about the calculation of redundancy payments, see IDS Employment Law Handbook, 'Redundancy' (2008), Chapter 6.

Expiry of fixed-term contract

The expiry of a fixed-term contract amounts to a dismissal under S.95(1)(b) ERA. Consequently, the non-renewal of a fixed-term contract can give rise to a claim of unfair dismissal or redundancy (where the employee has the appropriate qualifying service of one year or two years respectively) in the normal way. However, the employer is not required to follow the Acas Code in these circumstances since 'the non-renewal of fixed-term contracts on their expiry' is specifically excluded from its scope (see the Forewords and para 1).

The expiry and non-renewal of a fixed-term contract will normally be categorised as a dismissal for redundancy or 'some other substantial reason' (SOSR), and the reasonableness of the dismissal will be considered in the same way as any other type of dismissal for one of those reasons. Procedural failings may render the dismissal unfair, but the compensation adjustment provisions in S.207A TULR(C)A will not apply (see Chapter 5 under 'Adjustment to tribunal awards'). Two examples where a failure to consider alternative employment made the dismissal unreasonable:

- **Oakley v Labour Party** 1988 ICR 403, CA: O was employed under a one-year fixed-term contract as a Sales and Marketing Officer by the Labour Party. Before her contract expired, her employer decided to restructure the department in which O was employed and this entailed the disappearance of her job together with the substitution of another post involving broadly similar though more extensive duties. When O was informed that her contract would not be renewed, she rejected an offer of a short-term contract and applied instead for the new post. O was interviewed for the post but was not appointed. She claimed unfair dismissal. The Court of Appeal found that although the reorganisation of the department was a substantial reason of a kind to justify dismissal, the Labour Party had enacted a 'charade' by interviewing O since it had no intention of employing her and had not acted fairly in failing to give her application proper consideration. It had already made up its mind to get rid of her and the restructuring was simply a pretext. It had acted unreasonably and the dismissal was therefore unfair

- **Rochdale Metropolitan Borough Council v Jentas** EAT 494/01: J, a temporary employee, was repeatedly re-engaged on a series of one-month contracts for a period of 20 months. When her final temporary contract came to an end, her employment terminated. A tribunal found that there was SOSR for the decision not to renew her contract, but that the dismissal was unfair because the employer had not considered whether suitable temporary work was available in another department. J had a substantial period of service, had moved from position to position, and had sought to obtain a permanent post with the employer. The EAT upheld this decision, while commenting that it was a 'one-off case on particular facts'.

(Note that under the Fixed-term Employees (Prevention of Less Favourable Treatment) Regulations 2002 SI 2002/2034 ('the 2002 Regulations'), employees with fixed-term contracts have the right to be informed by their employer of all permanent vacancies within the establishment in which they work – Reg 3(6).)

It must be borne in mind that the exclusion from the Code only applies to dismissals brought about by the expiry and non-renewal of the fixed-term contract. If the employer dismisses the employee for misconduct – or poor performance – *before* the expiry of such a contract, the dismissal will be for conduct – or poor performance – and the Code will apply as set out above.

What is unclear is whether the Code will apply to the non-renewal of a fixed-term contract on its expiry if the *reason for the non-renewal* is the employee's conduct or poor performance. We would argue that if the reason for a dismissal is misconduct or poor performance, the Acas Code should apply, regardless of whether the employee was a fixed-term or permanent employee. Indeed, it is arguable that applying a less exacting disciplinary standard to a fixed-term employee could amount to less favourable treatment under the 2002 Regulations.

The 2002 Regulations are not included in the list of jurisdictions in Schedule A2 to the TULR(C)A to which the compensation adjustment provisions in S.207A TULR(C)A apply (see Appendix 1). However, the unfavourable treatment of fixed-term workers can amount to indirect sex discrimination under the Sex Discrimination Act 1976, in which case S.207A will come into play (see Chapter 5 under 'Adjustment to tribunal awards'). In Whiffen v Milham Ford Girls' School and anor 2001 ICR 468, for example, the Court of Appeal held that a policy of selecting employees on fixed-term contracts for dismissal when faced with redundancies was indirectly discriminatory on the ground of sex since it had a greater impact on women teachers than on men.

Note that an employee on a fixed-term contract that has previously been renewed, or who has been re-engaged on a new fixed-term contract, will be treated as a permanent employee if he or she has amassed four years' continuous service – Reg 8. The only exception will be if employment for a limited term can be justified on objective grounds. For further details, see IDS Employment Law Supplement, 'Fixed-Term Work' (2003).

Other dismissals

As explained earlier, the Acas Code is limited in its scope and there are a number of potentially fair reasons for dismissal under S.98 ERA to which it does not appear to apply (although, unlike redundancy, the Code does not expressly exclude them). These are retirement, statutory ban and 'some other substantial reason'. What unites them is an absence of 'fault' on the part of the employee, taking them outside the 'disciplinary' arena. In such cases, reference should be made to the pre-2004 regime and to case law decided before the advent of the statutory dispute resolution procedures. However, in many cases the reasons for dismissal may overlap and employers should be wary of abandoning the Code altogether. Furthermore, even where it does not apply for the purposes of the compensation adjustment provisions in S.207A TULR(C)A, the Code nonetheless sets out general standards of good practice that may be relevant to the initial question of liability.

In this section we briefly consider each of the three types of dismissal mentioned above in relation to the procedure that should be followed prior to dismissal. For more detailed discussion of these types of dismissal, see IDS Employment Law Handbook, 'Unfair Dismissal' (2005).

Retirement

Retirement was introduced as a potentially fair reason for dismissal under S.98(2)(ba) ERA by the Employment Equality (Age) Regulations 2006 SI 2006/1031, which removed the upper age limit for claiming unfair dismissal but at the same time made it automatically fair to dismiss an employee on reaching retirement age provided certain procedures are followed.

The retirement provisions are contained in Ss.98ZA–98ZH ERA, as inserted by the Regulations. They provide that there will be a 'retirement' dismissal if the employee is aged 65 or over or has reached a normal retiring age of below 65 that is objectively justified; the employer has given the relevant notice that the contract will end on a particular date and the contract does end on that date; and the employer has informed the employee of his or her right to request to work beyond the retirement date and has heard any appeal against a refusal of that right. In these circumstances, reasonableness is not an issue as the dismissal is deemed to be fair.

An employee who has been dismissed before the retirement age, or under the age of 65 when there is no retirement age or the retirement age cannot be justified, will not have been dismissed on the ground of 'retirement'. In these circumstances, the employer will have to show another fair reason for dismissal (to which the Code may apply).

In some cases it is left to an employment tribunal to decide whether a dismissal is by reason of retirement. These are where the employer has notified the employee of his or her impending dismissal at least two weeks before retirement, but not six to 12 months beforehand as required by the procedure.

If a tribunal finds that there has been no retirement dismissal and the alternative reason for dismissal is one to which the Code applies, the employer is at risk of having a finding of unfair dismissal made against him. This is because the procedures set out in the Code are more extensive than those required under the retirement provisions. He also risks an increase in the amount of any compensation awarded – see Chapter 5 under 'Adjustment to tribunal awards'.

Retirement dismissals are discussed in more detail in IDS Employment Law Supplement, 'Age Discrimination' (2006), Chapter 5.

Statutory ban

'Statutory ban' is a convenient shorthand expression for the potentially fair reason for dismissal set out in S.98(2)(d) ERA, which is that the employee could not continue to work in the position which he or she held without contravention (either on the employee's part or on that of the employer) of a duty or restriction imposed by or under an enactment. The most common example is where the employee has lost his or her driving licence and driving is an essential part of the job.

It is for the employer to show that there is a statutory prohibition which makes it impossible for the employee to carry on in the same job. If successful, the employer will have established a potentially fair reason for dismissal, but that alone will not be conclusive of the issue of fairness. The tribunal will still have to consider whether the employer acted reasonably in dismissing: if the employer could, for example, easily change the employee's job so that he or she could do it legally, dismissal is likely to be unfair. It is clear that this involves elements of a fair procedure as set out in the Code, but since it is not generally a disciplinary issue, the Code is unlikely to apply. The exception would be where there is more than one ground for dismissal. Two examples:

- **Handforth v Olaf Olsen (Newmillerdam) Ltd** ET Case No.9012/79: H was a sales secretary who needed to drive. She held an Australian licence and obtained a provisional licence from the DVLC, but did not tell the employer that she was not qualified to drive on her own in the United Kingdom. This came to light when her company vehicle was damaged in a minor accident and an insurance claim was repudiated. The tribunal held that H's dismissal because of statutory ban was fair because she had misled her employer

- **Bryan v Kennerty Farm Dairies Ltd** EAT 584/87: a distribution manager lost his driving licence and the employer pleaded capability (not statutory ban) as the reason for dismissal. A tribunal thought that the real reason for dismissal was related to conduct, but found the dismissal fair. The EAT upheld the decision, but thought that the tribunal could equally well have found SOSR to be the reason for dismissal.

If the employer has made out the reason for dismissal – the existence of a statutory ban on the employee's continued employment in the job – a tribunal must decide whether he acted reasonably in dismissing for this reason. This will involve considering such matters as:

- the likely duration of the statutory ban

- whether it affects the whole or only part of the employee's work

- whether the employee can readily be redeployed

65

- whether the employee has been given an opportunity to express his or her views, and whether any suggestions made have been reasonably considered.

An example:

- **Madan v St Helens and Knowsley Community NHS Trust** ET Case No.2100813/01: M worked for the NHS Trust as a clinical medical officer. She also ran a slimming clinic separately from her work for the Trust. The Trust became aware that the General Medical Council (GMC) had referred complaints against her work at the slimming clinic to its Professional Conduct Committee. It agreed that she could continue to work, provided her work was monitored, pending the outcome of the GMC investigation. A few weeks later the GMC suspended M from practice and, believing it would be illegal for her to continue working, the Trust terminated her employment. She claimed unfair dismissal. The tribunal held that M was dismissed because of a statutory ban but that the dismissal was unfair because there was no consultation and no opportunity for A to explore alternatives.

Qualifications. Note that the absence of the required qualifications for performing work of the kind which the employee was employed to do can also be a fair reason for dismissal under S.98(2)(a) ERA. This usually occurs where someone is engaged on the understanding that he or she will acquire a particular qualification and then fails to do so. However, the qualifications required for a particular job are not fixed and unchanging, and dismissing an employee who previously qualified for the job but who has subsequently failed to acquire a new qualification can also be fair. That said, although employers may change their policy regarding staff qualifications, they must act reasonably towards those serving employees who do not meet the new criteria.

Some other substantial reason

Section 98(1)(b) ERA is a general catch-all category covering dismissal for 'some other substantial reason of a kind such as to justify the dismissal of an employee holding the position which the employee held'. It provides a residual potentially fair reason for dismissal (commonly known as 'SOSR') that employers can use if the reason for dismissal does not fall within the four specific categories in S.98(2).

The employer is required to show only that the substantial reason for dismissal was a potentially fair one. Once the reason has been established, it is then up to the tribunal to decide whether the employer acted reasonably under S.98(4) in dismissing for that reason. As in all unfair dismissal claims, a tribunal will decide the fairness of the dismissal by asking whether the decision to dismiss fell within the range of reasonable responses that a reasonable employer might adopt. Depending on the circumstances, this may involve such factors as whether the employee was consulted, warned and given a hearing, and/or whether the employer searched for suitable alternative employment.

SOSR is most often invoked where:

- the employer is trying to reorganise the business and/or change the terms and conditions of employment in some way

- the employer tries to protect his interests either by preventing employees from setting up in competition or by taking steps to avert a potential leakage of confidential information

- there has been third-party pressure to dismiss the employee

- a fixed-term contract has expired (see 'Expiry of fixed-term contract' above); or

- dismissal for 'economic, technical or organisational' reasons has followed a transfer of an undertaking.

Since most dismissals for SOSR do not involve any fault on the part of the employee, it follows that the Code will not usually apply. However, SOSR can include reasons containing elements of conduct or capability. In Wilson v Post Office 2000 IRLR 834 the Court of Appeal held that an employer had dismissed an employee for SOSR because his attendance record did not meet the requirements of the agreed procedure. Even though the employee's absences had been caused by ill health, the Court held that the tribunal had erred when it characterised this as a capability dismissal. And in Huggins v Micrel Semiconductor (UK) Ltd EAT 0009/04 the EAT upheld a finding that a dismissal was for SOSR when it was caused by a breakdown in trust and confidence related to the employee's conduct. In such a case it is arguable that the Code should apply, since H's conduct played a large part in his dismissal. Nevertheless, the employer's failure to warn him that his conduct or his failure to provide a medical report could lead to dismissal did not make the resulting dismissal unfair. That said, the circumstances of the case were unusual and we would argue that a lack of warning would rarely be acceptable.

4 Grievances

What is a grievance?

Procedural steps

As discussed in Chapter 1, the provisions of the revised Acas Code of Practice on Disciplinary and Grievance Procedures ('the Code') are less prescriptive than the statutory procedures that they replaced, and absent the draconian consequences. However, a failure to comply with them could nonetheless prove costly. An employer who unreasonably fails to comply with the grievance procedures contained in the Code risks an increase in the compensation awarded in subsequent tribunal proceedings brought by the employee if the complaint falls within one of the jurisdictions contained in the new Schedule A2 to the Trade Union and Labour Relations (Consolidation) Act 1992 (TULR(C)A) (see Appendix 1). Conversely, an employee risks a reduction in any compensation awarded if he or she fails to raise a written grievance about an issue that subsequently becomes the substance of an employment tribunal claim.

The award adjustment provisions – which are contained in S.207A TULR(C)A and discussed in Chapter 5 under 'Adjustment to tribunal awards' – only apply to claims brought under one of the jurisdictions listed in Schedule A2 and where 'a relevant Code of Practice applies'. Since para 1 of the Acas Code says that it 'is designed to help employers, employees and their representatives deal with disciplinary and grievance situations in the workplace', it is relevant only in cases involving discipline and grievance issues. Its application to disciplinary situations is discussed in Chapter 3. In this chapter, we consider its application to grievances.

Common law duty. It should be noted that while a failure to follow the grievance procedures in the Code does not impose liability on an employer (although it may lead to an adjustment to any compensation awarded), common law does: an employer's obligation to address an employee's grievances has been found to amount to an implied contractual term existing in all contracts of employment. The leading case is WA Goold (Pearmak) Ltd v McConnell and anor 1995 IRLR 516, EAT. M and R, the complainants, were employed as salesmen for a firm of wholesale jewellers. Their employer introduced a change to sales methods that would result in a substantial drop in their take-home pay. M and R raised concerns about the change and when their employer consistently failed to address them they resigned and claimed constructive dismissal. In upholding their claims, the EAT held that there was an implied term in a contract of employment that the employer would 'reasonably and promptly afford a reasonable opportunity to their employees

68

to obtain redress of any grievance they may have'. That decision was followed in Waltons and Morse v Dorrington 1997 IRLR 488, EAT, where D, a non-smoker, complained about having to work in close proximity to offices where colleagues were allowed to smoke. Her employer failed to adequately address the situation and she resigned, claiming constructive dismissal. The EAT upheld D's claim, finding that her employer was in breach of an implied term to provide a working environment that was reasonably suitable for the performance of her duties and was also in breach of the implied term affording a reasonable opportunity to obtain redress of a grievance as enunciated in Pearmak.

Note that the employee must articulate the grievance to the employer before such an obligation is triggered since an employer cannot deal properly and appropriately with a grievance if it has not been effectively communicated to him – Sweetin v Coral Racing 2006 IRLR 252, EAT.

Formal or informal action. There is no statutory obligation on employers or employees to attempt to resolve issues informally or through mediation, although it is recommended in both the Foreword to the Code and the accompanying Acas Guide, 'Discipline and grievances at work' ('the Guide') (neither of which form part of the statutory Code). The Guide points out that in organisations where managers have an open policy for communication and consultation, problems and concerns are often raised and settled as a matter of course (page 40). It recommends that employees aim to settle most grievances informally with their line manager. Alternative methods of dispute resolution, including mediation, are discussed in Chapter 7.

If an informal approach fails to resolve the issue, or the complaint is sufficiently serious, the employee may raise it as a formal grievance. The employer will then need to follow a procedure that complies with the new Acas Code as a minimum, although an employer's own policy can be more detailed. As outlined in Chapter 2, this may or may not be contractual. If there is a conflict between the Code and an employer's internal procedures, the Code should prevail.

What is a grievance?

Paragraph 1 of the Code defines grievances as 'concerns, problems or complaints that employees raise with their employers'. This is wider in scope than the definition of a 'grievance hearing' for the purpose of the right to be accompanied under S.13(5) of the Employment Relations Act 1999 (and referred to at para 34 of the Code), which is 'a hearing which concerns the performance of a duty by an employer in relation to a worker'. The range of issues that should be dealt with under the Code is therefore broader than those attracting the right to be accompanied (see below).

The Acas Guide gives the following examples (at page 41) of issues that may give rise to grievances, although the list is not exclusive:

- terms and conditions of employment

- health and safety

- work relations

- bullying and harassment

- new working practices

- working environment

- organisational change

- discrimination.

The question 'What is a grievance?' assumed paramount importance under the now-repealed statutory grievance procedures (GPs) and generated a large body of case law, since an employee's failure to first raise a grievance with the employer meant that he or she was barred from bringing a tribunal claim in respect of it. It is unclear how much of that case law remains valid, as the old definition of a grievance in Reg 2(1) of the Employment Act 2002 (Dispute Resolution) Regulations 2004 SI 2004/752 – 'a complaint by an employee about action which his employer has taken or is contemplating taking in relation to him' – differs from that contained in the Code. However, some of the general principles established under the old regime are likely to continue to apply since, although an employee will no longer be barred from bringing a tribunal claim if he or she has failed to first raise a grievance, the question of what amounts to a grievance remains crucial to the question of compensation. Under S.207A TULR(C)A, an unreasonable failure to raise a grievance before submitting a tribunal claim may lead to a reduction in compensation of up to 25 per cent if the claim is successful. Conversely, a failure by the employer to recognise a grievance and therefore follow the Code in respect of it, may lead to an uplift in compensation of up to 25 per cent if the employee is ultimately successful in his or her tribunal claim. (See further Chapter 5 under 'Adjustment to tribunal awards'.)

The following principles derive from cases brought under statutory GPs but are likely to remain relevant under the Code. (Note that it will no longer be necessary to differentiate between 'the grievance' and 'the basis for it', as was required under the statutory GPs.)

A resignation letter can amount to a grievance. In Shergold v Fieldway Medical Centre 2006 ICR 304 the EAT held that a resignation letter sent by an employee setting out general complaints about the practice manager at the GP surgery where she worked amounted to a grievance. It was not necessary to make it clear that the letter constituted a grievance or that every detail of the grievance be mirrored in a subsequent tribunal claim, provided there is sufficient information for the employer to understand the nature of the grievance.

A grievance does not have to state that it is a grievance. In Commotion Ltd v Rutty 2006 ICR 290, EAT, R, who had recently taken over the care of her granddaughter, made an informal request to work a three-day week. Following her employer's rejection of that request, she applied in writing for a variation in her working pattern under the flexible working provisions in S.80F ERA. Her application did not state or suggest that it was to be regarded as a grievance. C Ltd rejected R's flexible working request and, following an unsuccessful internal appeal, R resigned and claimed constructive dismissal. The EAT held that there was no reason why a written flexible working request could not amount to a statutory grievance and upheld R's complaint.

Indeed, it seems that even the employee does not need to view a complaint as a grievance in order for it to be one:

- **O'Connell v British Broadcasting Corporation** ET Case No.3300364/05: O brought tribunal claims for unfair constructive dismissal, unlawful deduction from wages and holiday pay. The employer contended that her claims were inadmissible as she had failed to raise a statutory grievance, but the tribunal rejected this argument. Although in O's mind she had not formally initiated a grievance procedure, she had sent numerous e-mails to her employer detailing her complaints.

However, the grievance must make some reference to the complaint:

- **Canary Wharf Management Ltd v Edebi** 2006 ICR 719, EAT: E, who suffered from asthma, brought claims of unfair constructive dismissal, disability discrimination and unlawful deductions from wages. The tribunal accepted that, prior to instituting proceedings, he had written a lengthy letter to the employer complaining about his working conditions, and that the letter was sufficient to amount to a grievance in respect of all of his claims. However, the EAT held that, although one should not adopt an unduly technical or formal approach, E's letter had made no reference to reasonable adjustments, less favourable treatment or specific medical conditions and could not be fairly said to have raised a grievance under the Disability Discrimination Act 1995.

Statutory questionnaires. The equality legislation contains provisions for the use of statutory questionnaires which enable employees who think they may have been discriminated against to obtain information from their employer. An employer's evasive reply or failure to respond to a statutory questionnaire entitles an employment tribunal to draw inferences that the employer has committed an unlawful act of discrimination – see S.7B(4) Equal Pay Act 1970; S.74(2)(b) Sex Discrimination Act 1975; S.65(2)(b) Race Relations Act 1976;

S.56(3)(b) Disability Discrimination Act 1995; Reg 33(2)(b) Employment Equality (Religion or Belief) Regulations 2003 SI 2003/1660; Reg 33(2)(b) Employment Equality (Sexual Orientation) Regulations 2003 SI 2003/1661; Reg 41(2)(b) Employment Equality (Age) Regulations 2006 SI 2006/1031.

Under the old dispute resolution regime, a statutory questionnaire could not be relied upon as a statement of grievance – Reg 14 Employment Act 2002 (Dispute Resolution) Regulations 2004 SI 2004/752. However, no such exclusion is contained in the Code and there seems to be no reason why a questionnaire sent to the employer cannot constitute a grievance. Indeed, it may prove difficult to argue that it was *not* a grievance, since questions aimed at establishing whether discrimination has occurred surely come within the Code's definition of grievances as 'concerns, problems or complaints'.

An employer who fails to reply to a statutory questionnaire or to treat it as a grievance to which the Code applies will be vulnerable both in terms of liability (on the basis that an adverse inference of discrimination may be drawn) and of quantum (on the ground that an unreasonable failure to comply with the Code may lead to an increase in compensation of up to 25 per cent). Conversely, an employer who responds to a questionnaire by holding a grievance meeting and otherwise complying with the Code will, provided he addresses each aspect of the complaint, have dispelled any adverse inferences and avoided an uplift in compensation. However, an employer who responds in writing to a questionnaire but fails to treat it as a grievance will still be vulnerable to a compensation adjustment, although it is arguable that the tribunal may view non-compliance in these circumstances as reasonable.

A grievance can be raised by the employee's agent. In Arnold Clark Automobiles Ltd v Stewart and anor EAT 0052/05 S resigned after being replaced as general manager following his company's acquisition by ACA Ltd. His solicitor sent a 'without prejudice' letter to the new company alleging, among other things, that replacing A as general manager without consultation and discussion amounted to a breach of the implied term of trust and confidence entitling him to resign and claim unfair constructive dismissal. The letter further stated that 'unless matters can be amicably resolved in early course, our client intends to pursue appropriate claims in the employment tribunal'. It then set out S's anticipated claims as well as the amount of compensation sought. The EAT confirmed the tribunal's decision that the letter amounted to a grievance because the solicitor was acting as S's agent. The fact that it was 'without prejudice' and was expressed in an aggressive manner did not prevent this from being the case. A similar conclusion was reached by the EAT in Mark Warner Ltd v Aspland 2006 IRLR 87, EAT.

It is not only solicitors' letters that can amount to a grievance. In Chard v Telewest Communications plc ET Case Nos.1401078/05 and 1401786/05 a tribunal accepted that a letter written to an employer by the claimant's chiropractor, in which the chiropractor emphasised that adjustments were required to the claimant's role, amounted to a statement of grievance.

A continuing complaint requires only one grievance. In Smith v Network Rail Infrastructure Ltd EAT 0047/07 the EAT held that an employer's alleged failure to make reasonable adjustments to assist a disabled employee in finding alternative employment was a continuing complaint of discrimination. The employee's grievance letter in relation to that complaint was therefore valid for the entire duration of the failure up until the date that tribunal proceedings were instituted, and was not limited to events that had occurred prior to the date of the letter.

A grievance relating to equal pay need not specify the comparators in order to comprise a valid grievance – Suffolk Mental Health Partnership NHS Trust v Hurst and others; Sandwell Metropolitan Borough Council and ors v Arnold and ors 2009 IRLR 452, CA.

Procedural steps

Considerations for drafting a grievance policy are covered in Chapter 2. The following section explains the procedures required by the Acas Code, which sets out five steps that should be followed 'without unreasonable delay'. They are:

- let the employer know the nature of the grievance
- hold a meeting with the employee to discuss the grievance
- allow the employee to be accompanied at the meeting
- decide on appropriate action, and
- allow the employee to take the grievance further if not resolved.

Written records. The Foreword to the Code of Practice advises employers to keep a written record of any grievances they deal with. According to the Guide (at page 42) these should include:

- the nature of the grievance
- what was decided and actions taken
- the reason for the actions
- whether an appeal was lodged
- the outcome of the appeal, and
- subsequent developments.

Records should be treated as confidential and be kept no longer than necessary in accordance with the Data Protection Act 1998. Guidance on the application of that Act can be found in the Information Commissioner's 'Employment Practices Code Part 2: Employment Records of Practice', which is available on the Commissioner's website (www.ico.gov.uk).

The Guide also suggest that copies of records of meetings should be given to the employee, including copies of any formal minutes. However, certain information may need to be withheld, in order, for example, to protect a witness.

Collective grievances. The Code does not apply to collective grievances that are raised on employees' behalf by trade union or other workplace representatives, which should be dealt with in accordance with the organisation's collective grievance process (para 45). This assumes the existence of a collective grievance process, which will not always be the case, and it is not clear to what extent the Code can be ignored where no alternative exists. (Note that collective grievances raised directly by the employees themselves are not excluded.)

Let the employer know the nature of the grievance

The Code states that 'if it is not possible to resolve a grievance informally employees should raise the matter formally and without unreasonable delay with a manager who is not the subject of the grievance' – para 31. It is unclear if this means that an employee must *always* raise the matter informally first – risking a reduction in compensation in any subsequent successful tribunal claim if he or she fails to do so – or whether it is simply there to encourage informal resolution wherever possible.

A formal grievance should be made in writing and should set out the nature of the grievance – para 31. However, it does not have to be in a particular form. As the case authorities above show, tribunals were encouraged not to take too technical an approach under the statutory GPs and a similar attitude is likely to be adopted under the new regime, particularly given that the Code is less prescriptive than the statutory regime. There is no requirement that the grievance be raised within a particular timescale.

The Acas Guide urges employees to stick to the facts and avoid language which may be considered insulting or abusive (page 44). It also suggests that employees who have difficulty expressing themselves may wish to seek help from trade union or other employee representatives or from colleagues.

If the grievance is against the line manager, the employee should be able to raise it with another manager or their HR department if there is one. The Guide points out that it would be helpful if the grievance procedure explains who the employee should approach in these circumstances (page 44). In small firms run by an owner/manager there may be no alternative manager to raise the grievance with. It is in the interests of such employers to make it clear that they will treat all grievances fairly and objectively.

Employers should be aware that a failure to allow an employee to raise a grievance with someone other than the subject of the complaint may in certain circumstances amount to a breach of trust and confidence. In GMB Trade Union v Brown EAT 0621/06 and 0442/06, for example, B was employed as a Regional Political and External Relations Officer. When the new Regional Secretary (RS) was appointed, he reviewed the priorities of the region with the result that B was required to give up her political duties and concentrate instead on the recruitment of new members. She raised a grievance with RS objecting to the change but it was not resolved. The next stage in the procedure required the grievance to be heard by RS. Since he was the source of the complaint, B asked to move directly to the third stage of the procedure. When RS consistently refused, even after B become unwell with occupational stress, B resigned and claimed constructive dismissal. The EAT upheld the tribunal's finding that the union's insistence on sticking rigidly to the procedure in these circumstances amounted to a breach of trust and confidence and B had been constructively dismissed.

Allow the employee to be accompanied

Depending on the nature of the grievance, an employee may have the right to be accompanied by a companion to a grievance hearing under S.10 of the Employment Relations Act 1999 – see Chapter 6. However, not every concern or issue raised by an employee as a grievance will qualify, as this only applies to hearings concerning grievances arising from legal duties owed by the employer. To use the example given in the Guide, most employers will not be under a legal duty to provide their workers with car parking facilities and a grievance about such facilities will not attract the right to a companion. However, a disabled worker who needs a car to get to and from work would probably be entitled to a companion as there may be an issue about whether the employer was complying with his legal duty to make reasonable adjustments under the Disability Discrimination Act 1995 (pages 47–48).

To avoid the risk of inadvertently denying a worker his or her right to be accompanied, employers may wish to adopt the recommendation in the Acas Guide that all workers be allowed to be accompanied at a formal grievance meeting whether or not the statutory right under the 1999 Act applies (page 48).

It would be good practice for the employer to inform the employee of his or her right to be accompanied when inviting him or her to attend the grievance meeting in the same way as the employer is required to do under para 10 of the Code in respect of disciplinary hearings. However, there is no corresponding provision in the Code specifically relating to grievances.

Hold a meeting

The Code states that employers should arrange for a formal meeting to be held without unreasonable delay after a grievance is received (para 32). Although

75

the Guide recommends that this be within five working days (page 45), there is no legal obligation for it to be heard within that timescale – and in some circumstances it is conceivable that 'without unreasonable delay' could require an even quicker response. Presumably what is 'reasonable' will depend on the nature of the grievance, the availability of the parties concerned and the need for any investigation.

Employers, employees and their companions should make every effort to attend the meeting (para 33). An unreasonable failure to do so by either of the parties could lead to a compensation adjustment being made under S.207A TULR(C)A if the employee later brings a successful tribunal claim – a fact that may act as an incentive for both employer and employee to meet to resolve the matter (see Chapter 5 under 'Adjustment to tribunal awards').

Paragraph 33 of the Code states that at the meeting the employee should be allowed to explain his or her grievance and how he or she thinks it should be resolved. It also requires consideration to be given to adjourning the meeting for any investigation that may be necessary.

The Guide suggests (at page 45) that employers:

- consider arranging for someone who is not involved in the case to take a note of the meeting and to act as a witness to what was said

- check whether similar grievances have been raised before, how they have been resolved, and any follow-up action that has been necessary. This allows consistency of treatment

- consider arranging for an interpreter where the employee has difficulty speaking English

- consider whether any reasonable adjustments are necessary for a person who is disabled and/or their companion

- consider whether to offer independent mediation (see Chapter 7).

Grievances about fellow employees. The Guide recommends that the first step in dealing with grievances against fellow employees be to talk privately to the individual about whom the complaint has been made (page 46). Employers should beware that such a discussion does not inadvertently become a meeting at which the employee would be entitled to be accompanied. This would happen, for example, if it becomes evident that there is an issue over which disciplinary action could be taken, or the employee who is the subject of the grievance raises issues that could themselves be the basis of a grievance. In such cases, an employer should end the discussion and arrange for a formal meeting at which the employee can arrange for a companion to be present.

Complaints about third parties. The Guide recommends that employers deal with complaints about third parties, for example, where the employee is working on a different site, in the same way as he would for employees in the same workplace, with the employer investigating it as far as possible and taking action if required. It recommends that the employer make it clear to any third party that grievances are taken seriously and action will be taken to protect his employees (page 41).

Decide on appropriate action

The Code requires that 'following the meeting' the employer decide what action, if any, to take and to communicate the decision to the employee in writing without unreasonable delay (para 38). The Guide recommends that the meeting be adjourned before a decision is taken, to allow time for reflection and proper consideration (page 50).

Paragraph 38 goes on to state that the decision should, where appropriate, set out what action the employer intends to take to resolve the grievance. The employee should be informed that he or she can appeal if not content with the action taken.

An employer should take account of the employee's desired outcome of the grievance, but ultimately must make a decision based on all the circumstances. In Barratt v Accrington and Rossendale College EAT 0099/06 the EAT held that a failure to dismiss the perpetrator of a physical assault did not amount to a breach of trust and confidence. The perpetrator, who was demoted with a significant cut in salary, had had a long unblemished record prior to the incident and showed a good deal of remorse. Furthermore, there had been considerable provocation from the complainant. The employer arranged to monitor future contact between the two and warned the perpetrator that any further improper behaviour on his part would be dealt with by instant dismissal.

Allow the employee to take the grievance further

An employee who feels that his or her grievance has not been satisfactorily resolved should appeal:

- in writing

- without unreasonable delay

- letting the employer know the grounds for the appeal (para 39).

The Code also requires the employer to:

- hear the appeal without unreasonable delay at a time and place which should be notified to the employee in advance (para 40)

- deal with the appeal impartially and wherever possible by a manager who has not previously been involved in the case (para 41)

- communicate the outcome to the employee in writing without unreasonable delay (para 43).

The employee has the right to be accompanied at an appeal hearing and the Guide recommends that the employer remind him or her of this right when inviting him or her to the hearing (page 51). In small organisations where there is no senior manager to hear an appeal, the Guide suggests that it could be heard by another manager, the owner, or, in the case of a charity, the board of trustees.

Overlapping grievance and disciplinary cases. The Code is not prescriptive about how employers should handle a grievance that an employee raises during a disciplinary process. It allows for the disciplinary process to be temporarily suspended while the grievance is dealt with or, alternatively, where the grievance and disciplinary issues are related, for both to be dealt with concurrently (para 44).

5 Failure to follow fair procedures

Unfair dismissal

Constructive dismissal

Breach of contractual procedure

Discrimination

Pregnancy and maternity

Adjustment to tribunal awards

In the previous chapters we looked at the disciplinary and grievance procedures that employers and employees should follow in accordance with the revised Acas Code of Practice on Disciplinary and Grievance Procedures ('the Code') and the standards of reasonableness established through case law. In this chapter we consider the consequences for employers and employees who fail to follow fair disciplinary or grievance procedures.

Even prior to the introduction of the (now-repealed) statutory dispute resolution procedures (SDRPs) in 2004, it was well established that a failure to follow fair procedures can impose liability on employers for unfair dismissal, constructive dismissal and, where the procedures are contractual, breach of contract. And if the procedures are themselves discriminatory, or are applied with discriminatory effect, an employer may be liable for discrimination under the equality legislation. These principles still apply, and are examined below.

Financial penalties for a failure to follow disciplinary and grievance procedures were imposed by the SDRPs in an attempt to encourage parties to resolve their disputes in the workplace. Such penalties have been maintained under the new regime, though in a more flexible form, in the shape of new S.207A of the Trade Union and Labour Relations (Consolidation) Act 1992 (TULR(C)A), which was introduced by the Employment Act 2008 with effect from 6 April 2009. This provision allows employment tribunals to adjust the amount of compensation awarded in the majority of cases for an unreasonable failure by either party to comply with the standards of fairness contained in the Acas Code. We consider the application of S.207 at the end of this chapter.

Unfair dismissal

The fairness or otherwise of a dismissal is determined in accordance with S.98 of the Employment Rights Act 1996 (ERA). This requires the employer to establish a potentially fair reason for dismissal under S.98(1) and (2) (e.g.

79

capability, conduct, redundancy or 'some other substantial reason') and the tribunal to consider 'whether in the circumstances (including the size and administrative resources of the employer's undertaking) the employer acted reasonably or unreasonably in treating it as a sufficient reason for dismissing the employee' under S.98(4). In Polkey v AE Dayton Services Ltd 1988 ICR 142 the House of Lords established that procedural fairness is an integral part of the test of reasonableness under S.98(4) and Lord Bridge set down the following procedural steps that will be necessary in the great majority of cases if an employer is to be considered to have acted reasonably in dismissing:

- in a case of *incapacity*, giving an employee fair warning and a chance to improve

- in a case of *misconduct*, investigating fully and fairly and hearing what the employee wants to say in explanation or mitigation

- in a case of *redundancy*, warning and consulting affected employees, adopting a fair basis for selection and taking reasonable steps to redeploy affected employees.

In addition, when determining the question of reasonableness (i.e. liability), the tribunal should have regard to the revised Acas Code of Practice in accordance with S.207 TULR(C)A – see, for example, Spence v Manchester United plc EAT 0285/04.

The Polkey case also overturned the 'no difference' rule first fomulated in British Labour Pump Co Ltd v Byrne 1979 ICR 347, EAT, that established that where there was a proven procedural irregularity in an otherwise fair dismissal – e.g. failure to consult before a redundancy – but it could be shown that carrying out the proper procedure would have made no difference to the decision to dismiss, the tribunal would be able to find the dismissal fair. In Polkey, the House of Lords rejected this approach for all but a tiny number of cases where it would be 'utterly useless' or 'futile' to carry out the omitted procedure. Their Lordships said that the likelihood that dismissal would have occurred in any event could not make an unfair dismissal fair; however, it would have an impact on the amount of any compensatory award, which could be reduced to reflect the chance that the employee would have been fairly dismissed shortly afterwards in any event.

The Employment Act 2002, which introduced the SDRPs, brought about a partial reversal of the Polkey decision with the insertion of new S.98A into the ERA. S.98A(2) ERA provided that a failure by the employer to follow a fair procedure other than the applicable statutory dismissal or disciplinary procedure (DDP) would not be regarded by itself as making a dismissal unfair if the employer could show, on the balance of probabilities, that he would have decided to dismiss the employee if that additional procedure had been followed. If the employer could overcome this hurdle – and there was no issue of substantive unfairness – the dismissal would be deemed fair despite the procedural failures committed by the employer. Thus, the 'no difference' rule was reinstated, albeit only in circumstances where the minimum obligations of the statutory procedures had been observed. The repeal of S.98A by the Employment Act 2008 has returned us to the Polkey position, in which it is no longer possible for an employer to invoke the 'no difference' argument when defending a failure to adopt a fair procedure, except in cases where following the required procedure would have been futile.

Cases where the EAT has held that the circumstances were exceptional enough to 'excuse' the employer from following the proper disciplinary procedure are rare. However, here are two examples:

- **MacLeod v Murray Quality Foods Ltd** EAT 290/90: M worked in MQF's factory, which was struggling financially. The factory received a large order from a new customer and it was a matter of some urgency that the order be executed on time. Tea breaks were cancelled until the order was completed. M ignored this instruction and, after being warned that he would be dismissed if he did not return to work, was dismissed. The tribunal found that the circumstances were sufficiently urgent to justify the employer issuing the instruction, even though tea breaks were provided for in M's contract. It found the dismissal fair. The EAT accepted that the procedure was flawed in that no investigation had been carried out. Nonetheless, it agreed with the tribunal's finding on the basis that M knew why he was being dismissed and he had the opportunity to make representations to the managing director. Referring to Polkey, the EAT said that the circumstances of the case were 'exceptional'

- **Ellis v Hammond and anor t/a Hammond and Sons** EAT 1257/95: E had received several warnings, including three formal written warnings, about her conduct and her work. Matters came to a head when she was asked to work harder and, in response, swore at her supervisor and started throwing things at another employee. After a further warning, she swore at everybody and left. She did not report for work the following week and was dismissed without the benefit of a final disciplinary hearing. The EAT upheld a tribunal's decision that E had been fairly dismissed, even though the employer had decided to dispense with a final disciplinary hearing. The EAT stressed that the correct question for the tribunal to ask was whether the decision not to hold a final disciplinary hearing was justified at the time of the dismissal, not in the light of being wise after the event.

The test for tribunals to use is an objective one: they must ask whether an employer, acting reasonably, could have made the decision that it would have been futile to follow proper procedures – Duffy v Yeomans and Partners Ltd 1995 ICR 1, CA.

Constructive dismissal

In order to bring an unfair (or wrongful) dismissal claim, an employee must have been dismissed. 'Dismissal' is defined in S.95 ERA and includes the situation where the employee terminates the contract, with or without notice, in circumstances such that he or she is entitled to terminate it without notice by reason of the employer's conduct. This form of dismissal is commonly referred to as 'constructive dismissal'.

In the leading case on this subject, Western Excavating (ECC) Ltd v Sharp 1978 ICR 221, the Court of Appeal ruled that the employer's conduct which gives rise to a constructive dismissal must involve a repudiatory breach of contract. As Lord Denning MR put it: 'If the employer is guilty of conduct which is a significant breach going to the root of the contract of employment, or which shows that the employer no longer intends to be bound by one or more of the essential terms of the contract, then the employee is entitled to treat himself as discharged from any further performance. If he does so, then he terminates the contract by reason of the employer's conduct. He is constructively dismissed.'

In order to claim constructive dismissal, the employee must establish that:

• there was a fundamental breach of contract on the part of the employer

• the employer's breach caused the employee to resign

• the employee did not delay too long before resigning, thereby affirming the contract and losing the right to claim constructive dismissal.

(Note that a constructive dismissal is not necessarily an unfair one – Savoia v Chiltern Herb Farms Ltd 1982 IRLR 166, CA.)

The Acas Code is silent as to whether it applies to constructive dismissal cases. However, if it does, employees will be expected to raise a grievance before resigning and an unreasonable failure to do so may mean that any compensation awarded in a successful tribunal claim will be reduced under S.207A TULR(C)A (see 'Adjustment to tribunal awards' below). The Code is also silent as to whether it applies post-employment. However, as explained in Chapter 1, until the courts have had a chance to rule on this matter, we would advise employees to assume that it does – see Chapter 1 under 'The Acas Code of Practice – when does the Code apply?'

Failure to address grievance. In WA Goold (Pearmak) Ltd v McConnell and anor 1995 IRLR 516 the EAT held that an employer's obligation to address an employee's grievance amounted to an implied contractual term existing in all contracts of employment. Thus, a failure by an employer to address an employee's grievance may itself amount to a breach of contract and entitle the employee to resign and claim constructive dismissal – and possibly result in an uplift to any subsequent tribunal award under S.207A TULR(C)A for a failure to comply with the Code.

A failure to respond to an employee's grievance can also amount to a breach of the implied term of mutual trust and confidence derived from the House of Lords' judgement in Malik and anor v Bank of Credit and Commerce International SA (in compulsory liquidation) 1997 ICR 606. In that case, their Lordships concluded that there was an implied contractual term that an employer 'will not, without reasonable and proper cause, conduct his business in a manner likely to destroy or seriously damage the relationship of trust and confidence between employer and employee'. A breach of that term will entitle the employee to treat his or her employment as at an end and bring a claim for constructive dismissal.

The application of the Malik test in relation to a failure to deal adequately with a grievance procedure was considered by the EAT in Abbey National plc v Fairbrother 2007 IRLR 320, in which F had raised a number of grievances alleging bullying, all of which were rejected. She resigned in response, claiming that her employer had failed to adequately investigate her grievances and that this amounted to a breach of the implied term of mutual trust and confidence giving rise to a constructive dismissal. The employment tribunal found serious flaws in the way in which AN plc had dealt with her allegations and upheld her claim. However, the EAT disagreed, finding that AN plc had had 'reasonable and proper cause' to dismiss the employee's grievance and, following the Malik test, this did not give rise to a constructive dismissal. It concluded that the employer's conduct must be shown to fall outside the range of reasonable responses since the test for reasonableness should be the same in constructive unfair dismissal cases as it is in unfair dismissal claims where the claimant has been expressly dismissed. The EAT, presided over by then-President Mr Justice Elias, reformulated that approach in Claridge v Daler Rowney Ltd 2008 ICR 1267 but came to the same conclusion that an employer's handling of a grievance procedure cannot be calculated or likely to destroy or seriously damage the relationship of trust and confidence between employer and employee – and thus establish a constructive dismissal – unless it is outside the range of reasonable responses. However, it concluded that this is assessed by focusing on the third limb of the Malik test – whether the conduct is calculated or likely to destroy or seriously damage the employment relationship, rather than the second limb of whether he had 'reasonable and proper cause' as found in Fairbrother. Elias P pointed out that unreasonable behaviour has never itself been enough to establish constructive dismissal; it must be behaviour that amounts to a fundamental breach of the employment contract.

The approach of both cases was doubted in Bournemouth University Higher Education Corporation v Buckland EAT 0492/08, where the EAT held that the question of whether the employer's conduct fell within the range of reasonable responses is not relevant when determining whether there is a constructive dismissal. Rather, it is something to be considered if the employer puts forward a potentially fair reason for dismissal when deciding whether dismissal was reasonable. In that case, B, a university professor, had alleged breach of trust and confidence when the university overturned marks he had given on students' exam papers without recourse to him. The EAT found that although this was a fundamental breach, it had been negated by an inquiry which upheld B's complaint. By the time he resigned, therefore, there was no breach of contract for him to accept and he was not constructively dismissed.

Unreasonable disciplinary sanction. A constructive dismissal can also arise from an employer's unreasonable disciplinary sanction. According to the EAT in Bates v Liverpool City Council EAT 0309/06, the test here is whether the sanction was 'disproportionate'. However, this case should be treated with some caution as the EAT refused to overturn the tribunal's decision that the sanction of demotion and a final written warning fell 'within the range of options open to a reasonable employer' (i.e. the test rejected by the EAT in Buckland above).

Two examples of procedural unfairness amounting to a breach of contract leading to constructive dismissal:

- the issuing of a final warning without investigation (Thackeray v Acequip Ltd EAT 0396/03), and

- the application of two written warnings given within a short space of time with no opportunity to appeal and where the employee had an unresolved grievance (Marshall v BCM Group plc EAT 0401/03).

Breach of contractual procedure

If a disciplinary or grievance procedure is contractual, a failure to follow it can amount to a breach of contract resulting in a claim for damages. Such claims can be brought in an employment tribunal if they arise or are outstanding on termination of employment – Employment Tribunal Extension of Jurisdiction (England and Wales) Order 1994 SI 1994/1624. In these circumstances the Acas Code applies (see Schedule A2 to the TULR(C)A, set out in Appendix 1), with the result that the compensation adjustment provisions in S.207A TULR(C)A will come into play – see 'Adjustment to tribunal awards' below.

The most common type of breach of contract claims heard by tribunals are wrongful dismissal claims (i.e. dismissals in breach of contract), which can include dismissals in breach of a contractual disciplinary procedure. There is no service requirement to bring such a claim so an employee who is dismissed in breach of contract without the year's service necessary to claim unfair dismissal will still be able to recover damages for wrongful dismissal.

Damages are calculated on the basis of putting the employee back into the position he or she would have been in if the employer had not dismissed in breach of contract but had carried out the contractual procedure and given proper notice. In Boyo v Lambeth London Borough Council 1994 ICR 727 the Court of Appeal held that damages for wrongful dismissal include the length of time it would have taken to complete the disciplinary procedure so that losses for a failure to follow a disciplinary procedure are equivalent to the amount of lawful notice plus the length of time it would take to follow the procedure. Two examples:

- **Gunton v Richmond-upon-Thames London Borough Council** 1980 ICR 755, CA: G was employed under a contract terminable at one month's notice and his contract also prescribed a procedure for the dismissal of employees on disciplinary grounds. The employer dismissed him for disciplinary reasons with one month's notice, but failed to follow the prescribed procedure. The Court of Appeal held that G had been wrongfully dismissed. The correct measure of damages was to compensate G (subject to his duty to mitigate his loss) for lost salary from the date of the unlawful notice until the expiry of one month's notice served on the day when the proper disciplinary procedure, if followed, would have been concluded

- **Dietmann v Brent London Borough Council** 1988 ICR 842, CA: D was summarily dismissed for what the employer alleged to be 'gross misconduct'. She was entitled to a hearing, which she was not given, under the disciplinary procedure incorporated into her contract and to eight weeks' contractual notice. The Court of Appeal held that D's conduct did not amount to gross misconduct on the true construction of the contractual disciplinary rules and she was therefore entitled to eight weeks' notice. Furthermore, the employer was in breach of contract in denying her a disciplinary hearing. It would have taken eight weeks to set up and hold a disciplinary inquiry, so the correct measure of damages was 16 weeks' net pay, less any benefits received.

It is not necessary for the tribunal to determine the possible outcome of a contractual procedure. In Focsa Services (UK) Ltd v Birkett 1996 IRLR 325, EAT, B had been employed for approximately six months when he was given a week's notice of termination of his employment. B's contract provided that he should receive a week's notice during his first two years of service. It also provided for a disciplinary procedure. The tribunal held that the company was in breach of contract as it had failed to follow a fair and proper procedure and but for that breach the employee would not have been dismissed. It went on to assess damages on the same basis as that used for calculating a compensatory award following a finding of unfair dismissal and awarded loss of earnings to the date of the tribunal hearing and a sum for future loss on the basis that B would be expected to find new employment after 26 weeks. The EAT held that

85

the tribunal had failed to give proper regard to the normal common law rules as to damages in cases of wrongful dismissal, under which the loss is limited to the sums payable to the employee had the employment been lawfully terminated under the contract. In the instant case the employee was dismissed and his only entitlement to damages was in respect of any failure by the employer to give sufficient contractual notice of the dismissal. It was irrelevant to consider what might have happened had a contractual disciplinary procedure been followed. The only exception was where the employment would have been extended by operating the disciplinary procedure, but there was no evidence in the instant case to suggest that the disciplinary procedure would have had that effect.

Injunctions

In Irani v Southampton and South West Hampshire Health Authority 1985 ICR 590 an employee successfully obtained an injunction preventing his employer from dismissing him without first exhausting the dispute resolution procedure set out in the terms of a national collective agreement that was incorporated into his contract of employment. And in Mezey v South West London and St George's Mental Health NHS Trust 2007 IRLR 244 the Court of Appeal upheld a High Court decision to grant an injunction to prevent an employer from suspending an employee from work pending disciplinary proceedings.

Discrimination

As we have seen above, an employer's failure to comply with the Acas Code of Practice and to treat employees fairly when taking disciplinary action or dealing with grievances can give rise to a number of legal actions. If the reason for the failure is discriminatory – e.g. based on sex, race, religion or belief, disability, sexual orientation or age – the employer may face a claim under the equality legislation. And since compensation for discrimination is unlimited, and subject to a potential uplift of 25 per cent if the tribunal considers the failure unreasonable, this could prove costly.

Two examples of discriminatory proceedings:

- **Aziz v Crown Prosecution Service** 2007 ICR 153, CA: A, an Asian Muslim solicitor with the CPS, was suspended after a complaint was received alleging that she had made inappropriate and offensive comments during conversations with members of the staff at a magistrates' court about the terrorist attack on the World Trade Centre. The suspension was lifted a week later but A was transferred to a different office. A subsequent report exonerated her of any wrongdoing. In upholding A's claim of race discrimination, an employment tribunal found that by commencing disciplinary proceedings against A and suspending her from duty, the CPS had acted in breach of its disciplinary code, which required it to carry out appropriate preliminary inquiries or to make reasonable attempts to establish the facts of the alleged misconduct before instituting disciplinary proceedings. It had also failed to advise A of her right to be accompanied. The tribunal also found that the CPS had made assumptions that the allegations had substance because of A's origins, whereas such an assumption would not have been made in respect of a white solicitor, and that she was thus treated less favourably on racial grounds. The Court of Appeal upheld the tribunal's findings of race discrimination

- **Wandsworth Borough Council v Warner** EAT 0671/04: W raised a grievance against a supervisor, E, which failed to achieve a successful reconciliation. Shortly afterwards, E brought complaints about W that he had 'touched her on the arm in an intimidating fashion' and 'invaded her space'. Two managers, L and M, then also made complaints that W had bumped into them. The allegations were investigated and no action was taken. However, W was then suspended while the Council investigated further complaints from two other members of staff, neither of which was pursued. W, though, remained on suspension and the Council decided to instigate disciplinary proceedings against him in relation to the allegations made by E, L and M. It dismissed him for gross misconduct. The EAT upheld the tribunal's finding that W had been less favourably treated on the ground of race in the way in which the disciplinary investigation was carried out in his case, as compared with the way the Council had treated a white employee in similar circumstances, and by the investigators who failed to approach their investigation objectively.

Instigating a disciplinary procedure because an employee has made a complaint of discrimination can amount to victimisation, although the tribunal must consider the reason why the procedure was implemented – London Metropolitan University v Henry EAT 0344/04.

An employer has a defence to a claim of discrimination if he can show that he took such steps as were reasonably practicable to prevent an employee from committing disciplinary acts – S.41 Sex Discrimination Act 1975; S.32 Race Relations Act 1976; S.58 Disability Discrimination Act 1995; Reg 22 Employment Equality (Religion or Belief) Regulations 2003 SI 2003/1660; Reg 22 Employment Equality (Sexual Orientation) Regulations 2003 SI 2003/1661; Reg 25 Employment Equality (Age) Regulations 2006 SI 2006/1031. In Caspersz v Ministry of Defence EAT 0599/05, a sex discrimination case, the EAT held that the test is whether the steps taken were reasonably practicable and not whether they were effective. It also confirmed that an equal opportunities policy can amount to a defence if it is conscientiously implemented. Since the MoD had implemented a Dignity at Work policy and

87

had taken steps as soon as it was aware of C's complaints of sexual harassment, it successfully established a defence.

An employer should consider making adjustments to procedures to remove any disadvantage to a disabled employee in order to comply with the duty to make reasonable adjustments under the Disability Discrimination Act 1995. In British Telecommunications plc v Pousson EAT 0347/04 the EAT held that an employer's use of a performance procedure in relation to a diabetic employee's attendance and performance, which were affected by his disability, amounted to disability discrimination.

Pregnancy and maternity

It is not unlawful to take disciplinary action against or dismiss an employee who is pregnant or on maternity leave as long as the reason is unrelated to her pregnancy or maternity leave. However, it is automatically unfair to dismiss a woman if 'the reason or principal reason for the dismissal is of a prescribed kind, or the dismissal takes place in prescribed circumstances' – S.99 ERA. The prescribed reasons/circumstances are set out in Reg 20 of the Maternity and Parental Leave etc Regulations 1999 SI 1999/3312 ('the MPL Regulations') and include reasons connected with:

- the pregnancy of the employee
- the fact that the employee has given birth to the child (but only where the dismissal ends the employee's ordinary or additional maternity leave)
- the fact that the employee took, sought to take or availed herself of the benefits of ordinary maternity leave
- the fact that the employee took or sought to take additional maternity leave
- the fact that the employee failed to return to work after a period of ordinary or additional maternity leave where the employer failed to notify her of the date on which the period would end and she reasonably believed that that period had not ended, or the employer gave her less than 28 days' notice and it was not reasonably practicable for her to return on that date.

Redundancy. If a woman on maternity leave is fairly selected for redundancy she has the right to be offered a suitable alternative vacancy if one is available – Reg 10 MPL Regulations. The alternative job must be suitable and appropriate and on terms and conditions not substantially less favourable than if she had continued in her previous contract. She is entitled to be offered alternative employment with her employer or his successor or an associated employer. This means in effect that she has priority over other employees for suitable alternative vacancies since the need for employers to offer alternative employment to other employees goes to the reasonableness of the subsequent dismissal but is not a statutory obligation.

The employer does not have to extend the period of consultation until the employee returns to work, as long as he has consulted her over any suitable vacancy that exists – Calor Gas Ltd v Bray EAT 0633/04.

Adjustment to tribunal awards

If a claim is brought under one of the jurisdictions listed in Schedule A2 to the TULR(C)A (see Appendix 1), the new S.207A allows the amount of compensation awarded to be adjusted by up to 25 per cent in the following circumstances:

● the claim concerns a matter to which a relevant Code of Practice applies

● the employer or employee has failed to comply with the Code

● the failure was unreasonable, and

● the tribunal considers it just and equitable in all the circumstances to make an adjustment – S.207A(2) and (3).

If it is the employee who has failed to comply, compensation can be reduced by up to 25 per cent; if it is the employer's failure, compensation can be increased by the same amount.

A 'relevant Code of Practice' for these purposes is one which relates exclusively or primarily to procedure for the resolution of disputes – S.207A(3). The only Code that currently applies under this provision is the revised Acas Code of Practice on Disciplinary and Grievance Procedures.

It is important to bear in mind that the Code potentially applies to cases brought under *any* of the jurisdictions listed in Schedule A2, which, as discussed in Chapter 1, covers a wide range of claims. Furthermore, the Code is aimed at encouraging compliance by both employers *and* employees, so an employee's failure to follow the Code in respect of disciplinary action brought by the employer or in respect of a grievance raised by him or her is as likely to lead to a compensation adjustment as a failure by the employer to follow the correct procedures.

Disciplinary procedures. The Code relating to disciplinary issues impacts on unfair dismissal claims in relation to both liability and remedy. The employer's compliance with the Code is a factor to be taken into account when determining the reasonableness of the dismissal in accordance with the statutory test under S.98(4) ERA – see S.207 TULR(C)A. Assuming the dismissal is found to be unfair, compliance by both employer and employee is then taken into account when determining whether there should be an adjustment to any award under S.207A TULR(C)A. Compliance is also relevant to the question of compensation where the disciplinary procedures result in a claim being brought under one of the other jurisdictions listed in Schedule A2 to the TULR(C)A, e.g. a claim for unlawful detriment or wrongful or discriminatory dismissal.

Grievance procedures. The provisions of the Code that deal with grievances do not impose liability on the employer but are relevant to both parties in relation to the adjustment of awards. This is because a claim does not arise from an employer's failure to follow a fair procedure itself, although an alleged failure to deal adequately with a grievance could be evidence of, for example, discrimination. Equally, a failure to deal adequately with a grievance may amount to a breach of contract leading to a constructive dismissal claim – see 'Constructive dismissal' above.

Unreasonable failure to comply

Since the Code itself sets out standards of reasonableness it seems somewhat odd that an adjustment can only be made where there has been an *unreasonable* failure to follow the Code. This implies that a failure to follow the reasonable standards may nonetheless be reasonable. In cases of unfair dismissal, it seems likely that adjustments in successful unfair dismissal cases will be fairly common. This is because, as mentioned above, a failure to follow the Code is relevant to the question of liability as well as remedy and may render the dismissal procedurally unfair under S.98(4) ERA on the ground that the employer has acted unreasonably in all the circumstances. It is difficult to envisage a situation in which a tribunal could find that an employer has acted unreasonably in failing to comply with the Code when deciding on liability but then go on to hold that that failure was reasonable when it comes to deciding whether there should be an uplift in compensation. And if it does, can it really be said that the dismissal was unfair in the first place? It seems that remedies hearings generally are likely to become more protracted in future as parties put forward arguments concerning the reasonableness or otherwise of a failure to follow the Code.

Just and equitable

Where there has been an unreasonable failure to comply with the Code, the tribunal may increase or reduce the award where it 'considers it just and equitable in all the circumstances to do so'. This terminology is very similar to that used under the old statutory dispute resolution procedures, so tribunals may well rely on case law decided under that regime when deciding the amount of adjustment, if any. However, it should be borne in mind that under the old regime the EAT resisted setting out general principles for establishing the amount of any adjustment – with His Honour Judge McMullen stressing in Butler v GR Carr (Essex) Ltd EAT 0128/07 that it is for the tribunal to do what it considers just and equitable in the circumstances and that there are 'unlimited matters' to be considered.

The following two issues will continue to be relevant under the new scheme:

Does the employer's culpability affect the amount of the adjustment? The EAT in Metrobus Ltd v Cook EAT 0490/06 allowed an uplift of 40 per cent (allowed at the time) for a 'blatant' breach of procedure, accepting the tribunal's view that the provision was 'more penal than compensatory in nature'. A similar approach was taken by another division of the EAT in CEX Ltd v Lewis EAT 0013/07 when it held that the reason for the employer's failure to complete a statutory disciplinary procedure was ignorance rather than deliberate disregard, and this entitled a tribunal to limit the uplift to 10 per cent (the minimum adjustment under the statutory procedures).

The EAT in Scotland adopted a different approach in Aptuit (Edinburgh) Ltd v Kennedy EAT 0057/06 when ruling that an employer's overall 'shoddy' treatment of a long-serving employee when dismissing her for redundancy did not merit a 40 per cent uplift. This was because the shoddy treatment did not relate to any failure to complete a statutory procedure – in that case the employer had failed to invite her to an appeal hearing. However, that approach has to be questioned, as the legislation allowed an uplift if it was just and equitable in *all* the circumstances. Similar wording is found in the Code.

Can the overall size of the award be taken into account? In Abbey National plc and anor v Chagger 2009 IRLR 86 the EAT thought that it could. It did not find fault with the tribunal's decision to reduce the uplift on an award of almost £2.8 million from the 10 per cent it had been considering to 2 per cent, as the higher amount would have resulted in the employer being penalised to the extent of almost £300,000 for a procedural failure. 10 per cent was the minimum adjustment allowable save in 'exceptional circumstances' that would make it 'unjust or inequitable'. The size of the award made the circumstances of this case exceptional, but it nonetheless established the broader principle that a tribunal can take into account the overall level of compensation when considering what adjustment to make.

6 Right to be accompanied

The right

The remedy

Disability Discrimination Act 1995

Sections 10 to 15 of the Employment Relations Act 1999 (ERelA), as amended by the Employment Relations Act 2004, give workers a statutory right to be accompanied by a trade union representative or a fellow worker at a disciplinary or grievance hearing. In this chapter we explain how the statutory right to be accompanied works.

The right

Under S.10 ERelA, where a worker is required or invited by his or her employer to attend a disciplinary or grievance hearing and the worker 'reasonably requests' to be accompanied at the hearing, the employer must permit the worker to be accompanied by one companion.

It should be noted that the statutory right to be accompanied benefits 'workers', which is a wider category of individuals than 'employees'. A 'worker' is defined by S.230 of the Employment Rights Act 1996 (ERA) as an individual who is employed under a contract of employment or who provides services personally under a contract with another party who is not a client or customer.

An employer's failure to allow a worker to be accompanied entitles the worker to claim compensation of up to two weeks' pay (subject to the statutory cap on a week's pay, currently £350). The provision of a right to be accompanied is also one of the recommendations contained in the revised Acas Code of Practice on Disciplinary and Grievance Procedures ('the Code') (available at www.acas.org.uk/drr). It follows that, in respect of employees only (the Acas Code does not apply to the wider category of 'workers'), an employer's failure to afford the right may lead to an uplift in any compensation awarded in an associated employment tribunal claim and, where relevant, will also be taken into account when determining the fairness of any dismissal – see Chapter 1.

The right to be accompanied may only be exercised in relation to a 'disciplinary or grievance hearing'.

Disciplinary hearing
A disciplinary hearing is defined in the ERelA as a hearing that could result in:

- the administration of a formal warning to a worker by the employer – S.13(4)(a)

- the taking of some other action in respect of a worker by the employer – S.13(4)(b); or

- the confirmation of a warning issued or some other action taken – S.13(4)(c) (this applies to appeal hearings).

The right to be accompanied does not apply to investigation meetings, informal discussions or counselling sessions. This is reflected in the non-statutory Acas Guide, 'Discipline and grievances at work' ('the Guide'), which accompanies the Code of Practice and is also available on the Acas website (www.acas.org.uk/drr). The nature of a meeting may change, however, and the Guide points out that if it appears during the course of a meeting that formal disciplinary action may be needed, this should be dealt with at a formal hearing at which the worker will have the right to be accompanied (page 24).

It is not always clear where an investigation stops and disciplinary action begins, nor is it always apparent what constitutes 'formal action'. Consequently, much of the litigation arising from the right to be accompanied has revolved around the definition of 'disciplinary hearing'. The following are examples:

- **Skiggs v South West Trains Ltd** 2005 IRLR 459, EAT: S, who was employed by SWT as a guard, was called to a meeting to discuss a complaint that had been made against him by a colleague. He refused to answer questions unless he was appropriately represented but SWT insisted that it was not a disciplinary hearing and denied his request to be accompanied. S claimed this was a breach of his S.10 rights. The EAT upheld the tribunal's decision that the meeting did not fall within the definition of a disciplinary hearing under S.13(4) ERelA, meaning that the right to be accompanied did not arise. The EAT accepted that, in light of the EAT's decision in London Underground Ltd v Ferenc-Batchelor (see below), it was the nature of the meeting itself – not the description either or both parties happened to attach to it, or its possible consequences – that determined whether that meeting took on the character of a disciplinary hearing. In this case, the EAT observed that the meeting, which S himself described as 'an investigatory interview', clearly started out as a factual inquiry outside the scope of S.13(4) and the essential question, which the tribunal had correctly considered, was whether this informal interview later transformed into a disciplinary hearing. In the EAT's view, whether that point of transformation had been reached must be a question of fact and degree for the tribunal to decide in each individual case. In this instance, the tribunal had been entitled to find that the meeting remained an investigatory interview even though the matters to be discussed could have led to some later disciplinary process against S

- **Heathmill Multimedia ASP Ltd v Jones and anor** 2003 IRLR 856, EAT: J and his brother were employed by HMA Ltd. The company called the two employees to a meeting and, owing to its financial difficulties, gave them notice of termination of their employment. Since the employees had been unaware of the reason for the meeting and had been given very little warning of it, they had not had the opportunity to ask to be accompanied. The employment tribunal found that the reason for dismissal was redundancy and that 'it was not appropriate therefore to follow the disciplinary route in dealing with this matter'. However, in the tribunal's view, it was clear that the meeting was nonetheless a 'disciplinary hearing' within the meaning of S.13(4)(b) – i.e. it was one which could result in 'the taking of some other action in respect of a worker by his employer'. The tribunal held that, since the meeting fell within that definition, J and his brother had been entitled to be accompanied at the meeting. Before the EAT, HMA Ltd argued that the wording of S.13(4) envisages not just any action being taken by the employer, but only 'disciplinary action'. It argued that, where the purpose of a meeting is simply to inform an employee that he or she is to be dismissed by reason of redundancy, it is not a hearing, still less a disciplinary hearing, within the S.13(4) definition. The EAT agreed with the employer's submissions and overturned the tribunal's decision. Although the employer's dismissal procedure had a variety of shortcomings, it was not a disciplinary procedure and the employees had no right to be accompanied

- **London Underground Ltd v Ferenc-Batchelor; Harding v London Underground Ltd** 2003 ICR 656, EAT: F-B argued that sanctions against him in the form of training, coaching or counselling, which were imposed by his employer at a meeting, amounted to 'the taking of some other action in respect of a worker by his employer' within the meaning of S.13(4)(b), thus rendering the meeting in question a 'disciplinary hearing' for the purpose of the right to be accompanied. The EAT, rejecting F-B's argument, noted that the version of the Acas Code of Practice in place at the time stated that 'informal warnings and/or counselling are not part of the formal disciplinary procedure', and concluded that such actions are not disciplinary in nature and do not trigger the right to be accompanied. The second issue for the EAT was whether 'informal oral warnings' issued to F-B and H by LU Ltd were actually 'formal warnings' within the meaning of S.13(4)(a). The EAT found that, since the purpose of an informal warning is to help an employee improve, one of its key characteristics was that it would 'fade and disappear naturally by the passage of time'. A warning given with a set time limit, on the other hand, would be a formal warning. Further, if an employer were to take an informal warning into account in subsequent disciplinary action then, since the warning would form part and parcel of a formal disciplinary procedure, it could no longer be considered an informal warning. Turning to the facts, the EAT noted that LU Ltd's disciplinary procedure provided that 'all oral warnings will be confirmed in writing and the employee will be informed that disciplinary action may be taken if the expected standards are not met or if a similar offence is committed within a defined time scale'. The EAT held that such warnings were essentially formal warnings. It followed that the meetings at which LU Ltd issued F-B and H with the warnings had been 'disciplinary hearings' for the purposes of S.13(4) and that, therefore, the employees should have been afforded the right to be accompanied

- **Winfield v Frances Clarke Ltd** ET Case No.2505448/02: W, a security guard for FC Ltd, was called to a 'staff interview' to discuss a complaint by a client. He asked FC Ltd if he could be accompanied at the meeting and was told he could not. His employment was terminated during the meeting. FC Ltd contended that there was a distinction between staff interviews and disciplinary hearings, but the tribunal did not accept that submission. An 'interview' during which a dismissal could be imposed was clearly a disciplinary hearing for the purposes of S.13(4). In the circumstances, FC Ltd had denied W his statutory right to be accompanied

- **Simpson v South West Trains Ltd** ET Case No.2303901/01: S complained that he had been denied the statutory right to be accompanied at an investigatory interview. The tribunal rejected his complaint, ruling that the interview did not constitute a disciplinary hearing to which the right to be accompanied applied. The refusal of S's wish to be accompanied was not an infringement of the ERelA.

It should be noted that, at the time the Heathmill and London Underground decisions discussed above were heard, the EAT did not have the power to hear appeals in respect of the right to be accompanied – see Refreshment Systems Ltd t/a Northern Vending Services v Wolstenholme EAT 0608/03. This appears to be due to an oversight of drafting when the rights were introduced, but does mean that the EAT was acting outside its powers when it handed down those judgments. That oversight had been corrected by the time Skiggs came before the EAT – see 'The remedy – appeals' below – and during the course of its considerations in that case the EAT explicitly approved the London Underground decision. However, the Heathmills judgment remains non-binding and purely indicative of how the EAT may determine a similar matter.

Grievance hearing
Section 13(5) ERelA states that a grievance hearing 'is a hearing which concerns the performance of a duty by an employer in relation to a worker'. The Government explained, in the explanatory notes to the Bill which became the ERelA, that it did not intend workers to be granted a right to be accompanied at hearings where trivial or minor complaints were being dealt

with, but only at hearings concerning grievances arising from legal duties owed by the employer.

This definition is echoed in the revised Acas Code, which states that the right applies to a grievance meeting 'which deals with a complaint about a duty owed by the employer to the worker' and that it would apply where, for example, the complaint is 'that the employer is not honouring the worker's contract, or is in breach of legislation' – see para 34. The accompanying Acas Guide also refers to contractual issues, stating: 'For instance, an individual's request for a pay rise is unlikely to fall within the definition, unless a right to an increase is specifically provided for in the contract or the request raises an issue about equal pay. Equally, most employers will be under no legal duty to provide their workers with car parking facilities, and a grievance about such facilities would carry no right to be accompanied at a hearing by a companion' (pages 47–48).

However, elsewhere in the Code grievances are more widely defined as 'concerns, problems or complaints that employees raise with their employers' – see para 1. There are, therefore, separate definitions of a grievance according to whether it concerns the worker's statutory right to be accompanied or, more generally, the fair treatment of employees. Taking as an example the removal of a car parking space, which would not attract the right to be accompanied unless it involved the withdrawal of a contractual entitlement, if an employee raised this as a formal grievance an employer would be well advised to follow the Acas Code, since it could certainly be defined as a 'concern, problem or complaint'. Although this may have no consequences, as there is no obvious actionable claim in itself, an employer's failure to treat the issue seriously could conceivably be part of a course of conduct leading to a constructive dismissal. The consequences of failing to follow the Acas Code are discussed further in Chapters 4 and 5.

Employers may be best advised to follow the suggestion in the Guide that: 'It is generally good practice to allow workers to be accompanied at a formal grievance meeting even when the statutory right does not apply' (page 48).

Reasonable request

The statutory right to be accompanied only applies where a worker 'reasonably requests to be accompanied at the hearing' – S.10(1)(b) ERelA. The question of when a request will be reasonable is not addressed in the legislation. The Acas Code states that what is reasonable will depend on the circumstances of the individual case, but that 'it would not normally be reasonable for workers to insist on being accompanied by a companion whose presence would prejudice the hearing nor would it be reasonable for a worker to ask to be accompanied by a companion from a remote geographical location if someone suitable and willing was available on site' – paras 15 and 36.

The request to be accompanied does not have to be made in writing. There is no such requirement in the ErelA, and the Guide confirms this to be the case (see pages 24 and 48).

The companion

Section 10(2A) ERelA provides that the companion is chosen by the worker but must be someone who falls within one of the categories listed in S.10(3). This specifies that a worker's companion may be:

- an employed trade union official

- an official of a trade union who is not employed by the union, but whom the union has reasonably certified in writing as having experience of, or as having received training in, acting as a worker's companion at disciplinary or grievance hearings; or

- another of the employer's workers.

Section 119 of the Trade Union and Labour Relations (Consolidation) Act 1992 (TULR(C)A) states that a trade union official is an officer of the union (or of a branch or section of the union) or a person elected or appointed in accordance with the rules of the union to be a representative of its members (or some of them).

As the tribunal noted in the following case, S.10(3) gives a worker the option of being accompanied by a union official who is from a union not recognised by the employer:

- **Dee v Graphical, Paper and Media Union** ET Case No.5000039/01: D, who was employed by GPMU, requested that B, a friend who was an official of UNISON, accompany her at a disciplinary hearing. D was a member of a different union, one which was recognised by the employer, but said that she had lost confidence in that union. GPMU refused to allow her to be accompanied by B, insisting that D either be accompanied by someone from her own union or allow the hearing to proceed in her absence. D left the hearing, which continued without her, and she was dismissed. GPMU refused to allow B to accompany D to an appeal hearing and no such hearing took place. D complained to an employment tribunal, which held that GPMU had been in breach of the then equivalent of S.10(2A) in failing to allow D to be accompanied by B during the disciplinary process. B was an official of a trade union within the meaning of S.119 TULR(C)A and UNISON had provided the necessary certification of B's experience and training as required by S.10(3) ERelA. The tribunal saw no reason why, if a worker happens to know an official who is prepared to represent him or her in a private capacity, that worker should not be permitted to be so accompanied.

There is no duty on a person's co-workers, or even on trade union officials, to act as a companion if they do not wish to do so.

A grievance or disciplinary policy, whether contractual or not, may allow for workers to be accompanied by individuals in addition to those listed in S.10(3); for example, a partner or family member. It is also important to note that an employer may be required to make adjustments to its existing policy for disabled workers – see 'Disability Discrimination Act 1995' below.

In exceptional circumstances where a disciplinary hearing could lead to dismissal with particularly far-reaching consequences, the decision of the High Court in R (on the application of G) v Governors of X School and anor 2009 IRLR 434, QBD, establishes that legal representation may be required. That case involved a music assistant, G, who was dismissed for sexual impropriety and abuse of a position of trust after kissing a 15-year-old male work experience student. Once the allegations were established, the school had a duty to report G to the Secretary of State to determine whether he should be entered on a register as being unsuitable to work with children. Consequently, G's entire career was at stake. The High Court referred to Article 6(1) of the European Convention on Human Rights, which provides that an individual has the right to a fair hearing in the determination of his or her civil rights and obligations or of any criminal charge against him or her. The Court held that, although the proceedings were not of a criminal nature, the serious nature of the allegations and the severity of the consequences meant that G should have been allowed representation by a lawyer at his hearings before the disciplinary and appeal committees of the school's governors.

This case contrasts with the High Court's earlier decision in Kulkarni v Milton Keynes Hospital NHS Trust 2008 IRLR 949. In Kulkarni, a junior doctor accused of misconduct involving inappropriate touching of a patient sought legal representation at his disciplinary hearing. His main argument, that a right to legal representation could be implied into his contract of employment, was rejected by the High Court. The Court also rejected the alternative argument – which found favour in the case referred to above – that such a right derived directly from Article 6. The Court doubted that Article 6 was even engaged at disciplinary level and considered that, in any event, fairness was ensured by the possibility of a legally represented appeal to the General Medical Council and further to the employment tribunal.

The different judges sitting in each case were careful to confine their judgments to the particular facts before them and so nothing significant should be inferred from the different results. One key factor that may have made the difference is that, in Kulkarni, the claimant's contract of employment expressly excluded the right to legal representation. Arguably, a similar clause might have defeated the claimant's argument in R (on the application of G) v Governors of X School and anor (see above). However, given that the High Court in that case was prepared to allow legal representation contrary to the employer's clear policy and the normally authoritative Acas Guidance, it is not unthinkable that Article 6 may trump even an express contractual clause if fairness requires it.

Role of the companion

The Employment Relations Act 2004 clarified the role of the companion at hearings by inserting a new provision into the 1999 Act. Accordingly, S.10(2B) of the amended ERelA specifies that the employer must permit the worker's companion to:

- address the hearing in order to put the worker's case, sum up that case and respond on the worker's behalf to any view expressed at the hearing

- confer with the worker during the hearing.

However, S.10(2C) states that the employer is not required to permit the worker's companion to:

- answer questions on behalf of the worker

- address the hearing if the worker indicates that he or she does not wish the companion to do so

- prevent the employer from explaining his case or prevent any other person at the hearing from making a contribution.

The Acas Guide states that: 'It is good practice to allow the companion to participate as fully as possible in the hearing, including asking witnesses questions' (pages 26 and 49).

Rescheduling hearings

In order to ensure that the companion has a reasonable opportunity to attend, the employer must reschedule a disciplinary or grievance hearing for another time proposed by the worker where:

- the worker has a right to be accompanied under S.10

- the worker's chosen companion would not be available at the time proposed for the hearing by the employer; and

- the worker proposes an alternative time which is reasonable and which falls before the end of the period of five working days beginning with the first working day after the day proposed by the employer – S.10(4) and (5).

A 'working day' for these purposes is any day other than a Saturday or Sunday, Christmas Day or Good Friday, or a bank holiday under the Banking and Financial Dealings Act 1971 in that part of Great Britain – S.13(6).

99

Time off

Companions are entitled to paid time off during working hours to accompany a worker provided he or she is employed by the same organisation – S.10(6) ERelA. The amount of time off is that which the tribunal considers 'reasonable in all the circumstances having regard to any relevant provisions of a Code of Practice issued by Acas' – see S.168(3) TULR(C)A, which is extended to workers acting in the capacity of a companion by S.10(7) ERelA. According to the Acas Guide, as well as granting enough paid time off to cover the hearing it is good practice for the employer to allow time for the companion to familiarise him or herself with the case and confer with the worker before and after the hearing (pages 25 and 49). The right to payment for time off is governed by S.169 TULR(C)A, which applies in this context by virtue of S.10(7) ERelA.

The remedy

The enforcement provisions for workers in respect of their statutory right to be accompanied are contained in Ss.11 and 12 ERelA. Workers can complain about the refusal of the right, and both workers and their companions are protected against detriment and dismissal for asserting their rights. A worker who has been refused time off for acting as a companion or refused payment for it has a remedy under the TULR(C)A.

Denial of right to be accompanied

Section 11(1) ERelA entitles a worker to complain to an employment tribunal where his or her employer has failed, or threatened to fail, to:

- allow the worker's chosen companion to attend a hearing in accordance with S.10(2A)

- permit the companion to address the hearing or confer with the worker in accordance with S.10(2B)

- reschedule a disciplinary or grievance hearing in accordance with S.10(4).

Section 11(2) provides that such a complaint must be presented before the end of the period of three months beginning with the date of the failure or threat, or, where the tribunal is satisfied that it was not reasonably practicable for the complaint to be presented within that three-month period, within such further period as the tribunal considers reasonable.

A worker who succeeds in a claim brought under S.11(1) is entitled to an award of compensation up to a maximum of two weeks' pay and subject to the upper limit on a week's pay provided for by S.227(1) ERA (currently £350) – S.11(3)–(5). The calculation date for the purpose of calculating a week's pay is:

- in the case of a claim brought in conjunction with an unfair dismissal claim, the date on which the employer's notice of dismissal was given or, if no notice was given, the effective date of termination, and

- in any other case, the date on which the relevant hearing took place (or was to have taken place) – S.11(4).

Refusal of paid time off for a companion

Section 168(4) TULR(C)A (which applies in this context by virtue of S.10(7) ERelA) provides that a worker can present a complaint to an employment tribunal if his or her employer has failed to permit him or her to take time off to act as a companion. The worker can also present a tribunal complaint under S.169(5) TULR(C)A if the employer has failed to pay him or her for time off. In either case, the complaint must be issued within three months of the date when the failure occurred or, where the tribunal is satisfied that it was not reasonably practicable for the complaint to be presented within that period, within such further period as the tribunal considers reasonable – S.171 TULR(C)A. Where a tribunal upholds a complaint that a worker has been denied the right to time off it must make a declaration to that effect and may award such compensation as it considers just and equitable in all the circumstances having regard to the employer's default and to any resulting loss sustained by the worker – S.172(1)–(2) TULR(C)A. Where a tribunal finds that a worker has not been paid for the time off, it shall order the employer to pay the amount which it finds that he or she is due – S.172(3) TULR(C)A.

Protection against detriment and dismissal

The provisions contained in S.12 are designed to protect both the workers directly involved in disciplinary or grievance hearings and any co-workers chosen to accompany them.

Detriment. Section 12(1) provides that a worker has the right not to be subjected to any detriment by any act, or any deliberate failure to act, by his or her employer on the ground that the worker:

- exercised, or sought to exercise, the right to be accompanied under S.10(2A) or (2B) or the right to have a hearing rescheduled under S.10(4); or

- accompanied, or sought to accompany, another worker (whether of the same employer or not) pursuant to a request under S.10.

Under S.12(2), S.48 ERA applies to a detriment under S.12(1). This means that it will be for the employer to show the ground on which any act, or deliberate failure to act, was done.

Dismissal. Section 12(3) provides that a worker's dismissal will be automatically unfair for the purposes of Part X of the ERA where that worker is dismissed on the ground that he or she:

101

- exercised, or sought to exercise, the right to be accompanied under S.10(2A) or (2B) or the right to have a hearing rescheduled under S.10(4); or

- accompanied, or sought to accompany, another worker (whether of the same employer or not) pursuant to a request made under S.10.

Section 12(4) further provides that the qualifying period contained in S.108 ERA does not apply to unfair dismissal claims arising from the right to be accompanied. Further, S.12(6) extends the unfair dismissal rights contained in the ERA, which are normally restricted to those who meet the definition of 'employee', to workers in these circumstances. In addition, S.12(5) extends the availability of interim relief, provided for by Ss.128–132 ERA, to such dismissals.

Appeals

As mentioned above, the EAT originally had no jurisdiction to hear an appeal from a decision of an employment tribunal relating to the right to be accompanied at a disciplinary or grievance hearing – Refreshment Systems Ltd t/a Northern Vending Services v Wolstenholme (above). However, this was rectified by the Employment Relations Act 2004, which amended S.21 of the Employment Tribunals Act 1996 to give the EAT jurisdiction to hear such appeals.

Disability Discrimination Act 1995

There may be additional obligations in relation to companions that go beyond those in the statutory scheme explained above. S.4A of the Disability Discrimination Act 1995 imposes a duty on employers to make reasonable adjustments to prevent physical features of premises, or other arrangements applied by or on behalf of an employer (referred to as provisions, criteria or practices), from placing a disabled person at a substantial disadvantage. An employer may be expected to modify arrangements in relation to disciplinary and grievance hearings in order to comply with S.4A. Para 5.20 of the Disability Rights Commission Code of Practice: Employment and Occupation (2004) gives the example of a woman with a learning disability who might, owing to a reasonable adjustment, be allowed to take a friend who does not work with her to act as an advocate at a grievance hearing. It goes on to suggest that the employer may have to ensure that the meeting is conducted in a way that does not disadvantage or patronise the disabled woman.

Similarly, the Acas Code suggests that reasonable adjustment may be needed for a worker with a disability at a disciplinary or grievance hearing, and possibly for the worker's companion if he or she is disabled. It gives as an example 'the provision of a support worker or advocate with knowledge of the disability and its effects' (pages 25 and 48).

For more details about disability discrimination, see IDS Employment Law Handbook, 'Disability Discrimination' (2002).

7 Alternative dispute resolution

Background

Mediation

Judicial mediation

Acas services

A culture change?

Alternative dispute resolution (ADR) refers to methods of resolving disputes with the help of a neutral third party that do not involve litigation (whether before a court or a tribunal). They are seen by many as the best way of achieving early dispute resolution and are used widely outside the employment field to deal with family and civil law disputes (e.g. commercial and construction). However, thus far, take-up for employment disputes has been limited.

In this chapter we briefly discuss the reasons for this and how, following the repeal of the statutory dispute resolution procedures (SDRPs), ADR is now being promoted for employment disputes. We then go on to describe the ADR techniques that are most appropriate in the employment context, namely mediation and Acas conciliation. Finally, we consider the likelihood of there being a 'culture change', involving a shift away from employment tribunal litigation and towards a focus on early dispute resolution, particularly through mediation.

Background

The revised Acas Code of Practice on Disciplinary and Grievance Procedures ('the Code'), which replaces the SDRPs, makes no mention of ADR (other than in passing in the Foreword) and there is no legal obligation or incentive to undertake it. However, the use of ADR, particularly in the form of conciliation and mediation, is being encouraged under the post-SDRP regime with the aim of resolving employment disputes as early as possible.

Gibbons Review
Michael Gibbons, a member of the Better Regulation Commission, set the ball rolling when the Government commissioned him to carry out a review of the dispute resolution and employment tribunal process in December 2006 (the 'Gibbons Review'). His report, 'Better Dispute Resolution: A review of employment dispute resolution in Great Britain', published in March 2007, recommended ADR as an effective way of bringing about early resolution of employment disputes. He advocated promoting awareness of early resolution

methods and encouraging parties to find mutually acceptable solutions before resorting to litigation. However, he decided against recommending a similar approach to that adopted in New Zealand, i.e. a state-driven, near-mandatory use of ADR (see 'Comparison with other jurisdictions', below). He concluded instead that employers and employees should be encouraged to undertake ADR voluntarily. He suggested this could be done by:

- increasing the awareness of and demand for ADR services by promoting their benefits, and

- ensuring an adequate and timely supply of ADR services in order to meet increased demand.

Encouragement of ADR

As noted above, there is no legal impetus to undertake ADR under the post-SDRP regime: there is no mention of it in the main body of the Code and, consequently, there will be no adjustment of tribunal awards for failure to participate in some form of ADR. However, the Foreword to the Code does advocate the use of mediation, stating that where it is not possible to resolve disciplinary and grievance issues in the workplace, employers and employees should consider using an independent third party (either internal or external) to help resolve the problem. In addition, the accompanying 82-page non-statutory guide, 'Discipline and grievances at work' ('the Acas guide'), goes into some detail about the use of mediation. Further, the Government has allocated extra funds to Acas for it to provide services to help employers and employees resolve their disputes at an early stage – see under 'Acas services' below.

Employers willing to consider going down the ADR route can draw support from the proliferation of free advice available on how and when to implement alternative methods of dispute resolution. In addition to the information included in the Acas Guide, Acas has produced a booklet, 'Managing conflict at work' (ACAS/B19), with the stated aim of preventing future conflict in the workplace and minimising the impact of ongoing conflict. The booklet has been updated to take account of the April 2009 changes to the law. Acas has also produced a guide in conjunction with the Chartered Institute of Personnel and Development (CIPD), 'Mediation: An employer's guide' ('the Acas/CIPD guide'), aimed at promoting good dispute resolution techniques. Both of these, together with the Code and the Acas Guide, are available on the Acas website (www.acas.org.uk).

There is also information on the Department for Business, Enterprise and Regulatory Reform's website (www.berr.gov.uk) about 'non-legislative measures' that can be used to resolve disputes, and on the Government's public information website (www.direct.gov.uk). And the Equality and Human Rights Commission (EHRC) is also endorsing mediation as a means of resolving discrimination-related disputes (see www.equalityhumanrights.com).

Mediation

Mediation involves a neutral third party – the mediator – bringing two sides together with the aim of reaching a mutual agreement. Although the mediator is in charge of the process, he or she is not there to judge and any agreement reached comes from those in dispute, not the mediator. The mediation process will usually involve each side having the opportunity to describe the situation from their perspective and to listen to the other person, before moving on to look at ways in which the situation can be improved for the future or, failing that, to negotiate a mutually acceptable settlement to the claim. The fact that the employer will usually bear the cost of the mediation should not affect the neutrality of the mediator.

The Foreword to the Code states that mediators can be provided as part of an in-house mediation scheme: employees trained and accredited by an external mediation service can act as internal mediators in addition to their day jobs so long as they are not involved in the particular dispute at issue. Alternatively, the mediator can come from an external mediation provider (which will charge for its services). As well as public and not-for profit sector providers such as Acas and the Centre for Effective Dispute Resolution (CEDR), there are a growing number of private sector mediation providers offering workplace mediators and training for in-house mediators.

A much-trumpeted aspect of mediation is its confidentiality. The Acas/CIPD guide, for example, states that anything that happens during the mediation is confidential to the parties and cannot be used in future legal proceedings (except, for example, where disclosure is required by law). However, it is difficult, in a legal context, to envisage parties' commitment to confidentiality being taken on trust and the parties may wish to sign a mediation agreement committing to the mediation process and to confidentiality. CEDR offers a 'Model Mediation Agreement' stated to be 'without prejudice' and containing a number of clauses on confidentiality (see wwwcedr.co.uk). Further issues concerning the confidentiality and 'without prejudice' nature of mediation are discussed under 'Legal issues' below.

If mediation leads to settlement of the dispute, all agreed matters will typically be written down and signed by the parties. A 'Model Settlement Agreement' is available on CEDR's website.

Why use mediation?
As noted, there is no mention of mediation – or indeed any other form of ADR – in the main body of the Acas Code and there will therefore be no adjustment to any future tribunal award should the parties fail to attempt it – see further Chapter 5 under 'Adjustment to tribunal awards'. However, as stated above, it

105

was strongly promoted in the Gibbons Review and its use is advocated in the Foreword to the Code, as well as in the accompanying Guide.

Mediation is seen as a less burdensome process than formal litigation, and more likely to achieve the desired results. Even the successful party in a tribunal claim may not be entirely satisfied with the outcome, and the stress and cost of the tribunal proceedings may, in themselves, taint the result. The Gibbons Review referred to 'compelling evidence' that employees in certain discrimination cases find the experience of bringing an employment tribunal claim difficult, unpleasant and ultimately not a good solution to the original problem, even in cases where the claim is successful. Mediation, on the other hand, can lead to an outcome which satisfies both parties. According to the Gibbons Review, mediation offers a wider and more flexible range of outcomes than a tribunal verdict can deliver – e.g. an apology, a job reference or a change in behaviour – over and above the possibility of any financial settlement. In addition, as stated in the introduction to the Acas/CIPD guide, mediation is more likely to enable the employer to address the root cause of the problem and make changes to working practices that will benefit employees more generally in the long term. What is more, many advocates of mediation speak of 'ownership' of the dispute, in that the parties themselves are more fully involved in seeking an outcome they can accept.

Mediation is also seen as a good way of preventing conflict from escalating in the workplace. As noted in the introduction to the Acas/CIPD guide, an early intervention improves the likelihood of maintaining good and productive employment relations in the longer term, unlike the formal legal process, which, being essentially adversarial, tends to preserve hostility.

Further perceived advantages of mediation are its flexibility, in that it can be tailored to suit specific circumstances; its informality (the parties can be unrepresented, although the employee, in particular, may wish to have someone there for moral support); and its confidentiality, which can allow for a more open and honest discussion. These issues are discussed in more detail under 'Legal issues' below. In addition, mediation can be a cheaper and quicker alternative to tribunal claims. It is possible for disputes to be resolved in a single day without either side being represented, legally or otherwise. The Acas/CIPD guide emphasises the costs to employers of a tribunal claim, coupled with the initial resources spent on discipline and grievance procedures. It also cites indirect costs such as sickness absence, high staff turnover and negative publicity.

When to use mediation

Certain types of dispute are more suited to mediation than others. The Acas Guide and the Acas/CIPD guide give the examples of relationship breakdown, bullying and harassment, perceived discrimination, personality clashes and communication problems. Grievances – as opposed to disciplinary issues – perhaps most obviously lend themselves to mediation. Part 3 of the Acas/CIPD guide explains that managers may not always see it as appropriate to surrender their discretion in relation to disciplinary issues where they believe a point of principle is at stake, such as misconduct or poor performance. However, some might argue that the 'point of principle' issue applies equally to grievances, as seen from the employee's point of view. In any event, the Foreword to the Code states that mediation should be considered for both grievance and disciplinary issues. Furthermore, as the Acas Guide explains, the line between disciplinary and grievance issues may in specific instances become blurred, in which case the employer may prefer to tackle the underlying relationship issues by means of mediation rather than impose a disciplinary sanction (page 8).

Mediation is seen as being especially effective when used at the initial phase of any disagreement, before conflict escalates. The introduction to the Acas/CIPD guide states that early intervention can prevent both sides becoming entrenched and their differences turning into a full-blown dispute. Nonetheless, the Acas Guide states that mediation can be used at any stage in the conflict provided any ongoing formal disciplinary or grievance procedures are suspended. It can even be used 'to rebuild relationships after a formal dispute has been resolved' (page 7).

The Acas/CIPD guide envisages mediation techniques being used by managers as part of their day-to-day approach in dealing with conflict, noting in Part 5 that mediation will be most effective if it is consciously introduced as part of an organisation's approach to people management and reflected in its culture, policies and processes. However, employers should still be wary of going to mediation too early. The Acas Guide states that mediation may not be suitable as a first resort. Rather, people should be encouraged to speak to each other and talk to their manager before they seek a solution via mediation (page 8). The Guide goes on to note other situations in which mediation will not be appropriate:

- when a manager seeks to use it to avoid his or her managerial responsibilities

- when a decision about right or wrong is needed (for example, where there is possible criminal activity)

- when the individual bringing a discrimination or harassment case wants it investigated

- when the parties do not have the power to settle the issue

- when one side is completely intransigent and using mediation will only raise unrealistic expectations of a positive outcome.

107

We would suggest that certain other kinds of dispute are also inapt to be dealt with by way of mediation. For example, where there are clear and relatively straightforward legal points at issue, such as disputes over wages or holiday pay, mediation is unlikely to provide a solution. In addition, disputes over redundancies would be difficult to resolve, and serious cases of bullying and harassment and clear cases of discrimination may need to be dealt with by more formal procedures. That said, part 3 of the Acas/CIPD guide makes the point that although there are situations where it may not be appropriate to use mediation, it is often not clear-cut and each case should be judged on its merits.

Legal issues

Despite mediation's perceived informality and flexibility, there is a danger that it could, in certain circumstances, become legalistic, or at least more formal. There are various legal and quasi-legal considerations that those contemplating mediation should consider.

Use of representatives. The Acas/CIPD guide states that the use of representatives (legal or otherwise) is not encouraged in mediation and that the involvement of lawyers could formalise the process and shift the emphasis from joint problem-solving to negotiating the best deal for the respective parties. However, according to CEDR's Model Mediation Procedure, professional advisers, particularly lawyers, can and usually do attend the mediation and play an important role in:

- the exchange of information and opinion on fact, evidence and law

- supporting their clients in the negotiations

- advising clients on the implications of settlement

- drawing up the settlement agreement and any consent order.

'Morally binding'. Many sources talk of mediation being 'morally binding' and having 'no legal status'. However, as explained above, the law cannot be divorced completely from mediation and, with that in mind, it is difficult to envisage parties' commitment to issues such as confidentiality and settlement being taken on trust. In a legal context, there is no room for moral obligations and it is not surprising that some mediation providers, such as CEDR, require the parties to enter into confidentiality agreements prior to undergoing mediation. This, of course, adds somewhat to the formality of the process.

Binding written agreements. Mediated settlement agreements lack the finality of compromise agreements which, provided certain statutorily prescribed conditions are satisfied, allow employees to contract out of their statutory employment rights – effectively barring them from bringing proceedings in respect of claims to which the compromise agreement relates – in return for a financial settlement. There is, therefore, a potential danger that an employee may bring a claim in respect of a dispute the employer thought had been settled via a mediated agreement. It is, of course, possible for mediation to lead to a valid compromise agreement binding the parties and preventing a tribunal claim being brought based on the complaint. However, for this to happen, lawyers would need to be involved in the process, if only to give formal sign-off to the agreement. For further details about compromise agreements, see IDS Employment Law Handbook, 'Employment Tribunal Practice and Procedure' (2006), Chapter 9.

'Without prejudice'. There is also the danger that if mediation is not successful, things said or written during the mediation process may become highly relevant in any future tribunal proceedings. The Acas/CIPD guide asserts that what happens during the mediation cannot be used in future legal proceedings without agreement from both parties and that, in practice, courts prefer to protect the confidentiality of the mediation process because they realise that otherwise, people would be less willing to use mediation. In the context of civil claims at least, what goes on in the course of a mediation is, with some exceptions, treated as being privileged (meaning it cannot be referred to or relied upon in subsequent court proceedings) on the basis that it is 'without prejudice'. There have, however, been no reported employment cases on this specific point and it is therefore difficult to say for certain how tribunals and courts will approach the issue.

Nevertheless, there have been a number of employment decisions on the 'without prejudice' rule more generally. For the rule to be engaged, there has to be a 'dispute' between the parties, notwithstanding that litigation has not yet begun. In Barnetson v Framlington Group Ltd and anor 2007 ICR 1439 the Court of Appeal held that a 'dispute' occurs when the nature of the exchanges is such that the parties contemplate or could reasonably be expected to contemplate litigation if they do not agree. According to the EAT in BNP Paribas v Mezzotero 2004 IRLR 508, raising a grievance does not necessarily mean that parties to an employment relationship are 'in dispute': a grievance might be upheld, or alternatively dismissed, for reasons that the employee finds acceptable, in which case the parties never reach the stage where they could properly be said to be 'in dispute'.

Therefore, it cannot be said with any certainty that mediation will always be conducted on a 'without prejudice' basis, especially if it is being used early on' before any legal claim has crystallised. As explained below under 'Acas services', Acas mediation (as opposed to conciliation) is only available if a tribunal claim is 'unlikely'. If a tribunal claim is unlikely, it might be difficult to argue that the parties are, at that stage, contemplating litigation.

109

Judicial mediation

In June 2006 the Employment Tribunals Service launched a 12-month pilot 'judicial mediation scheme' in three employment tribunals (Newcastle, Birmingham and London Central). 'Judicial mediation' involves disputing parties being brought together to mediate by the employment tribunal during the course of proceedings. As with all mediation, the mediator remains neutral and helps the parties to reach their own settlement but does not make a decision about the case or give opinions. Strictly speaking, it might be argued that judicial mediation doesn't exactly constitute ADR since it involves an element of litigation – at the very least, the submission of a tribunal claim form.

The pilot scheme targeted certain more complex race, sex and disability discrimination cases. According to the Consultation Paper, 'Transforming tribunals: Implementing Part 1 of the Tribunals, Courts and Enforcement Act 2007', conflict with Acas's statutory role in conciliation (see 'Acas services', below) was avoided by forwarding to Acas details of cases where parties expressed interest in judicial mediation and by building a slight delay into the process so that Acas could make further attempts to help the parties settle prior to going to tribunal.

Following this pilot, S.7B was inserted into the Employment Tribunals Act 1996 by the Tribunals, Courts and Enforcement Act 2007, which came into force in November 2008. This section envisages a role for judicial mediation in employment tribunal proceedings, allowing for regulations to be made to provide (by means of practice directions) for tribunal panel members (whether wing members or employment judges) and employment tribunal (and other tribunal) staff to act as mediators in relation to disputed matters in a case that is subject to proceedings – S.7B(1) and (4). Perhaps surprisingly, S.7B(2) allows a tribunal panel member to act as a mediator even if he or she has been selected to decide matters in the case. S.7B(3) does, however, go on to provide that once a member has begun to act as mediator, that member may only decide matters in the case with the consent of all the parties.

Although this is not expressly stated in S.7B, judicial mediation will presumably be voluntary, with both parties required to be in agreement before it can go ahead, as was the case with the pilot scheme. As yet, no regulations or practice directions have been issued under this section.

Acas services

Following the Gibbons Review, the Government is investing resources in Acas with the aim of providing new services to help employers and employees resolve their disputes at an early stage. It was announced in

February 2008 that Acas would receive an extra £37 million in funding over three years to enable it to support the reform of dispute resolution. The Acas helpline (08457 47 47 47) is being bolstered by an increase in the number of advisers, additional training for advisers and extended hours (8 am to 8 pm Monday to Friday and 9 am to 1 pm on Saturday). There are also a number of other projects aimed at increasing the number of employment disputes that are kept out of the tribunal system.

Conciliation

A new, more proactive early dispute resolution service – pre-claim conciliation (PCC) – was launched across Great Britain by Acas on 6 April 2009. This PCC service is aimed at resolving disputes before they even enter the tribunal system. The guidance produced by Acas on its conciliation service notes that the key features of conciliation are that it is voluntary, free, impartial, independent and confidential. The service is largely accessed through the Acas helpline and will usually be conducted over the telephone. In relevant cases, a helpline adviser will refer an issue to an Acas conciliator where it appears to the adviser that there is a potential tribunal claim that has not been issued.

The PCC service was piloted in Manchester, Newcastle and Nottingham between June and November 2008. According to 'Pre-Claim Conciliation pilot: Evaluation summary report', 903 referrals were made for PCC during the pilot. Based on a sample survey of these cases, the report found that around a third were settled and a further 39 per cent were not progressed further. The report also found that requests for referrals were more likely to come from lower paid, less skilled occupations in small organisations without an HR function or a trade union presence.

The PCC service is offered as part of Acas's general power to conciliate both before and after tribunal proceedings have been instituted. When a claim is lodged at an employment tribunal, a copy of the ET1 claim form is sent to Acas so that it can contact the parties involved and offer its conciliation services. As mentioned in the 'Acas annual report and accounts' for 2007/08, Acas is developing a case-flow system in partnership with the Tribunal Service to enable case papers to be sent to Acas electronically and provide for electronic case management of both tribunal and Acas conciliation cases. This is intended to ensure that Acas conciliators get case papers more quickly than in the past and are able to start conciliation earlier. According to the report, Acas hopes to complete the roll-out of the system during 2009/10 (having piloted it later in 2008/09).

Tribunal claim 'likely'. According to the Acas booklet, 'Managing conflict at work' (ACAS/B19), conciliation is aimed at disputes where a claim to an employment tribunal is *likely* or has been made' (our emphasis). The booklet goes on to say that conciliation is the same as mediation except that it takes

111

place against the backdrop of an actual or potential claim to an employment tribunal. It therefore follows that PCC will only be offered by Acas if there is a potential tribunal claim. According to BERR, disputes that employees and employers have been unable to resolve by other means (such as internal grievance, discipline or appeal procedures) and which are likely to give rise to an employment tribunal claim if third party help is not provided, may be suitable for early conciliation. This can be contrasted with mediation (see above), which can be used in the early stages of a dispute to nip it in the bud.

Power to conciliate. Sections 5 and 6 of the Employment Act 2008 amended S.18 of the Employment Tribunal Act 1996, replacing Acas's *duty* (in certain circumstances) to seek to conciliate before proceedings have been instituted with a *power* to conciliate. (Note, however, that Acas still retains a duty to seek to conciliate *after* a tribunal claim has been submitted, a duty which now subsists throughout tribunal proceedings rather than for a fixed period – see Chapter 1 under 'Consequential amendments – Acas conciliation' for further details.)

Acas has produced a short guidance note – 'Conciliation in cases that could be the subject of employment tribunal proceedings after 6 April 2009' – explaining how it intends to respond to requests (or proactively seek) to exercise its power to conciliate in potential employment tribunal claims. It explains that it will seek to make conciliation available in any dispute that is otherwise likely to be the subject of a tribunal claim subject to the following considerations:

- the employer and employee must already have made reasonable efforts to resolve the issues, for instance by using the organisation's grievance or disciplinary procedures

- there must be grounds to believe that a valid claim is likely to be made (i.e. there is a prima facie cause of action, the employee appears eligible to make the claim and there is not already a binding agreement to settle the matter)

- where providing conciliation in individual claims could risk undermining collective and/or other agreements and procedures, it will generally be inappropriate

- if the volume of potential claims exceeds its capacity, Acas will prioritise cases, generally focusing on those in which the employment relationship can be preserved and those which would tend to lead to longer hearings

- it will endeavour to identify potential claims where employment relationships have not yet broken down permanently, where early conciliation could be particularly useful

- from time to time, other considerations may also need to be taken into account, such as the comparative cost to Acas of exercising its power to conciliate in different cases and the likely prospect of resolution if it does so.

The Gibbons Review also suggested that disputes involving small and medium-sized employers might be targeted because they are likely to have fewer in-house resources for dispute resolution.

Exceptions. Acas is of the view that PCC should be focused on the types of claims that tend to lead to longer hearings (such as those concerning workplace discrimination) in preference to claims that tribunals can usually dispose of quickly (such as those for unauthorised deductions from wages or disputes over holiday pay). Thus, it intends – at least initially – to provide PCC in respect of all potential claims *except* those which concern only unpaid wages or unauthorised deductions, breach of contract, redundancy payments or holiday pay. However, it will provide pre-claim conciliation in multiple claims covering any of these jurisdictions where it appears that there are collective employment relations implications. Acas hopes to be able to broaden pre-claim conciliation to all jurisdictions once it has completed a programme of recruitment and training later in 2009

Outcome of conciliation. When parties choose to go down the route of conciliation, the object of the process is to reach a settlement that binds both parties and prevents the employee from bringing or continuing a claim based on that particular complaint. If a settlement is agreed, this will generally be recorded on a standard form known as a COT3. However, it is not necessary that an Acas-conciliated settlement agreement be in writing – Gilbert v Kembridge Fibres Ltd 1984 ICR 188, EAT. Nevertheless, if the agreement is oral, it must be established that the technical requirements of contract law have been satisfied in order for the agreement to be legally binding – Duru v Granada Retail Catering Ltd EAT 281/00.

Once a settlement has been reached, all tribunal claims are barred in respect of the claim (or potential claim) which is being settled – see S.203 ERA (and equivalent provisions in other statutes). Therefore, an employee's only remedy, in the event of the employer's failing to honour his side of an agreement reached via conciliation, will be for breach of contract. For further details of Acas conciliation, see IDS Employment Law Handbook, 'Employment Tribunal Practice and Procedure' (2006), Chapter 9.

Acas mediation

Acas also has its own mediation service (see above for details of mediation). The Acas booklet, 'Managing conflict at work', explains that mediation will be available from Acas in cases where no claim to an employment tribunal is likely. Unfortunately, the distinction between cases where a tribunal claim is likely and those where a claim is unlikely will not always be obvious. The distinction matters because Acas charges for its mediation service, unlike its conciliation service, which is free. The guidance, 'Mediation explained: How Acas can help', explains that where someone has a complaint about his or her employment rights which he or she could take to an employment tribunal, help is offered free of charge (i.e. conciliation), but if the conflict or dispute has not got that far then a charge is made for mediation. The Acas Annual Report for 2007/08 states that charged mediation will be offered where the parties indicate no wish to seek judicial determination of the difference between them.

Acas Arbitration Scheme

The Acas Arbitration Scheme was introduced on 21 May 2001 in England and Wales, and extended to Scotland in 2004. The scheme, which is voluntary – both parties must agree to refer the dispute to arbitration – is intended to provide a faster, non-legalistic, more cost-effective and informal alternative to employment tribunals for the resolution of *unfair dismissal* and *flexible working* disputes (i.e. disputes arising out of an employee's application for a change in his or her terms and conditions of employment made under S.80F ERA). No other kind of complaint can currently be dealt with under the scheme. The scheme is contained in the Schedules to the ACAS Arbitration Scheme (Great Britain) Order 2004 SI 2004/753 – for unfair dismissal – and the ACAS (Flexible Working) Arbitration Scheme (Great Britain) Order 2004 SI 2004/2333 – for flexible working. Arbitration differs from mediation in that it involves a third party actually making a decision about the case, whereas in mediation the third party's role is to help the parties to reach a resolution themselves.

Although the scheme has a number of advantages as compared to the traditional forum of an employment tribunal, it also has disadvantages that may put off one or both sides – for example, the fact that there is a very limited right of appeal. In fact, the scheme has not proved particularly popular so far. By 31 March 2008, Acas had accepted a total of 60 cases for resolution since the scheme's inception. The Acas Annual Report for 2007/08 notes that the number of cases received has not fulfilled expectations.

Further information about the Acas scheme can be found in IDS Employment Law Handbook, 'Employment Tribunal Practice and Procedure' (2006), Chapter 9. In addition, a detailed explanation of the scheme can be found in the Acas Booklets, 'The ACAS arbitration scheme for the resolution of unfair dismissal disputes: A guide to the scheme' and 'The ACAS arbitration scheme for the resolution of flexible working disputes: A guide to the scheme'.

A culture change?

Only time will tell how effectively mediation will fit into the arena of employment disputes. It will certainly require a sea change in the way employment disputes are currently handled. Michael Gibbons envisaged a 'culture change', with the parties to employment disputes thinking in terms of

114

finding ways to achieve an early outcome that works for them, rather than in terms of fighting their case at a tribunal. The question that has to be asked is whether the current system is sufficiently flexible to allow this to happen.

Mediation does not sit particularly easily with the disciplinary and grievance procedures contained in the Acas Code of Practice on Disciplinary and Grievance Procedures that must be followed if the parties are to avoid a potential adjustment of up to 25 per cent to any tribunal award. Nor does mediation tie in well with the three-month time limit that applies to most employment tribunal claims. Indeed, both these factors could pose a potentially significant hindrance to mediation in employment disputes. The Gibbons Review made the point that the three-month time limit means that even where employees want to resolve matters informally they may feel under pressure to get the formal process underway. Given that the parties will be mindful of the need to comply with the Acas Code or risk a potential adjustment in compensation, their main priority will be to follow the procedures set out in the Code, rather than to undergo mediation, which forms no part of those procedures.

Even if the parties do commit to mediation, they will still be mindful of the three-month limitation period and of the need for the employee to protect his or her position. This, in itself, introduces an undesired legal element to mediation. Thus, it appears that, despite what the Acas Guide says about mediation being possible 'at any stage in the conflict' (page 7), it may not be particularly suitable for disputes that have crystallised into potential claims. The point at which this happens will, of course, not always be obvious and lawyers may need to be consulted, particularly on borderline cases, to advise on the nature and merits of the conflict and thus whether mediation is appropriate in the circumstances. This could undermine the perceived informality of mediation.

Under the current system, therefore, mediation is probably of most use at the first signs of conflict, when it becomes clear that there may be a problem and that an informal 'chat' will not be sufficient to resolve it. However, this relies heavily on the employee being sufficiently motivated and/or confident to raise a complaint at a point when conflict is only brewing under the surface. No doubt employers will also be encouraged to watch out for signs of conflict between employees and to intervene where necessary by seeking informal resolution and offering mediation in appropriate cases. However, such a proactive approach may not come easily for some.

Comparison with other jurisdictions

There has been something of a culture shift in family and civil law disputes, which have seen an increased use of ADR, particularly mediation, in recent years. However, these situations are not directly comparable to employment

115

disputes as the use of ADR in these jurisdictions is far more entrenched. For example, Lord Woolf's civil procedure reforms went much further to encourage the early settlement of disputes through ADR by instigating a combination of pre-action protocols, active case management by the courts and cost penalties for parties who unreasonably refused to attempt negotiation or consider ADR.

In countries such as New Zealand, the use of mediation to resolve employment disputes has significantly increased. However, the Gibbons Review points out that there, mediation is state-backed and virtually mandatory. As noted in the Northern Ireland government consultation document, 'Resolving workplace disputes', in New Zealand there is a legal presumption that ADR should take place in employment disputes: although not required to do so, the parties are generally expected to attempt mediation (which is offered free by the state) as a first step once a dispute has escalated beyond the workplace. Further, an unresolved dispute will generally go to New Zealand's Employment Relations Authority for further investigation before it goes to tribunal. The Authority must consider whether attempts have been made to resolve the problem by mediation and will direct the parties back to mediation if it thinks fit. Tribunal proceedings will only ensue if the investigation stage does not resolve the dispute. The Gibbons Review cited good reasons for not instigating a similar near-mandatory approach in Great Britain, including cost and the fact that mediation could then become too procedural and legalistic. These are legitimate concerns. However, it has to be questioned whether 'encouragement' of mediation mainly though promotion can achieve the desired culture change.

Appendix 1

Tribunal jurisdictions listed in Schedule A2 to the Trade Union and Labour Relations (Consolidation) Act 1992 (TULR(C)A)

An unreasonable failure to comply with the Acas Code of Practice on Disciplinary and Grievance Procedures in respect of a successful claim brought under any of these jurisdictions may lead to an adjustment to the compensatory award under S.207A TULR(C)A:

- equal pay – S.2 Equal Pay Act 1970

- discrimination on all prohibited grounds (sex, race, disability, sexual orientation, religion or belief, and age) – S.63 Sex Discrimination Act 1975; S.54 Race Relations Act 1976; S.17A Disability Discrimination Act 1995; Reg 28 Employment Equality (Sexual Orientation) Regulations 2003 SI 2003/1660; Reg 28 Employment Equality (Religion or Belief) Regulations 2003 SI 2003/1661; Reg 36 Employment Equality (Age) Regulations 2006 SI 2006/1031

- inducements relating to trade union membership or activities – S.145A TULR(C)A

- inducements relating to collective bargaining – S.145B TULR(C)A

- detriment in relation to trade union membership and activities – S.146 TULR(C)A

- detriment in relation to union recognition rights – Para 156 of Sch A1 to TULR(C)A

- unauthorised deductions and payments – S.23 Employment Rights Act 1996 (ERA)

- detriment in employment – S.48 ERA

- unfair dismissal – S.111 ERA

- redundancy payments – S163 ERA

- detriment in relation to the national minimum wage – S.24 National Minimum Wage Act 1998

- breach of contract arising on termination of employment – Employment Tribunal Extension of Jurisdiction (England and Wales) Order 1994 SI 1994/1623/ Employment Tribunal Extension of Jurisdiction (Scotland) Order 1994 SI 1994/1624

- breach of the Working Time Regulations – Reg 30 Working Time Regulations 1998 SI 1998/1833

- detriment relating to European Works Councils – Reg 32 Transnational Information and Consultation of Employees Regulations 1999 SI 1999/3323

- detriment in employment under Reg 45 of the European Public Limited-Liability Company Regulations 2004 SI 2004/2326

- detriment in employment under Reg 33 of the Information and Consultation of Employees Regulations 2004 SI 2004/3426

- detriment in employment under para 8 of the Schedule to the Occupational and Personal Pension Schemes (Consultation by Employers and Miscellaneous Amendment) Regulations 2006 SI 2006/349

- detriment in relation to involvement in a European Cooperative Society – Reg 34 European Cooperative Society (Involvement of Employees) Regulations 2006 SI 2006/2059

- breach of the Cross-border Railways Working Time Regulations – Reg 17 Cross-border Railways Services (Working Time) Regulations 2008 SI 2008/1660.

Appendix 2

Tribunal jurisdictions listed in Schedule 5 to the Employment Act 2002 (EA 02)

Under S.38 EA 02 successful claims brought under any of these jurisdictions entitle the claimant to recover compensation where the employer failed to provide the claimant with a statement of his or her employment particulars as required under S.1 of the Employment Rights Act 1996 (ERA):

- equal pay – S.2 Equal Pay Act 1970

- discrimination on all prohibited grounds (sex, race, disability, sexual orientation, religion or belief, and age) – S.63 Sex Discrimination Act 1975; S.54 Race Relations Act 1976; S.17A Disability Discrimination Act 1995; Reg 28 Employment Equality (Sexual Orientation) Regulations 2003 SI 2003/1660; Reg 28 Employment Equality (Religion or Belief) Regulations 2003 SI 2003/1661; Reg 36 Employment Equality (Age) Regulations 2006 SI 2006/1031

- inducements relating to trade union membership or activities – S.145A TULR(C)A

- inducements relating to collective bargaining – S.145B TULR(C)A

- detriment in relation to trade union membership and activities – S.146 TULR(C)A

- detriment in relation to union recognition rights – Para 156 of Sch A1 to TULR(C)A

- unauthorised deductions and payments – S.23 ERA

- detriment in employment – S.48 ERA

- unfair dismissal – S.111 ERA

- redundancy payments – S163 ERA

- detriment in relation to the national minimum wage – S.24 National Minimum Wage Act 1998

- breach of contract arising on termination of employment – Employment Tribunal Extension of Jurisdiction (England and Wales) Order 1994 SI 1994/1623/ Employment Tribunal Extension of Jurisdiction (Scotland) Order 1994 SI 1994/1624

- breach of the Working Time Regulations – Reg 30 Working Time Regulations 1998 SI 1998/1833

- detriment relating to European Works Councils – Reg 32 Transnational Information and Consultation of Employees Regulations 1999 SI 1999/3323

- detriment in employment under Reg 45 of the European Public Limited-Liability Company Regulations 2004 SI 2004/2326

- detriment in employment under Reg 33 of the Information and Consultation of Employees Regulations 2004 SI 2004/3426

- detriment in employment under para 8 of the Schedule to the Occupational and Personal Pension Schemes (Consultation by Employers and Miscellaneous Amendment) Regulations 2006 SI 2006/349

- detriment in relation to involvement in a European Cooperative Society – Reg 34 European Cooperative Society (Involvement of Employees) Regulations 2006 SI 2006/2059

- breach of the Cross-border Railways Working Time Regulations – Reg 17 Cross-border Railways Services (Working Time) Regulations 2008 SI 2008/1660

- detriment in relation to special negotiating body or employee participation under Reg 51 of the Companies (Cross-Border Mergers) Regulations 2007 2007/2974.

Appendix 3

Transitional provisions – BERR example scenarios to illustrate where the statutory DDPs or GPs continue to apply

Dismissals (involving disciplinary/dismissal procedure):

- Mrs A is issued with a step 1 letter on 15 March 2009 and is dismissed on 5 April 2009. On 4 July 2009 she has reasonable grounds for believing that the dismissal procedure is being followed and receives a 3 month extension until 4 October with the case being heard at an employment tribunal during December 2009 – the pre-6th April 2009 regime (the 'old regime') applies as on or before 5th April 2009 the employer had taken a step under the standard dismissal and disciplinary procedure

- Mr B is dismissed on 6 April 2009, his employer had issued a step 1 letter in March 2009. Mr B makes an unfair dismissal claim on 6 May 2009 with the claim being heard at an employment tribunal in June 2009 – old regime applies as on or before 5th April 2009 the employer had taken a step under the standard dismissal/disciplinary procedure

- Miss C is dismissed on 6 May 2009, the employer had issued a step 1 letter on 6 April 2009. She makes an ET1 claim for unfair dismissal on 4 July 2009 with the case being heard by an employment tribunal during September 2009 – new regime applies as employer took action on or after 6 April 2009.

Employer takes action which forms the basis of a grievance with a 3 month time limit, e.g. a discrimination claim:

- employer takes action on 10 January 2009 which continues beyond 6 April 2009. Mrs D submits a written grievance on 7 April 2009. The case is heard at an employment tribunal in December 2009 – old regime applies as where an act begins on or before 5 April 2009 and continues, and the grievance is put in before 4 July, the old regime applies

- employer takes action on 10 January 2009 which stops on 10 February 2009. Mr E submits a written grievance on 11 February 2009 and makes an ET1 claim on 7 April 2009 - old regime applies as the act takes place before 6 April 2009

- employer takes action on 10 January 2009 which continues until 9 January 2010. Miss F submits a written grievance on 10 January 2010 and makes an ET1 claim – new regime applies as although Miss G may have had grounds for a grievance before 6 April 2009, the written grievance has been made (or ET1 presented) after 4 July 2009

- employer takes action on 5 April 2009 which continues until 5 May 2009. Mr G submits a written grievance on 5 July 2009, makes an ET1 Claim on

4 October 2009 and the case is heard by an employment tribunal in January 2010 – new regime applies as written grievance submitted (or ET1 presented) after 4 July 2009

- employer takes action on 6 April 2009 which continues until 5 November 2009. Mr H submits a written grievance on 6 November 2009, makes an ET1 claim on 4 May 2010 and the case is heard during June 2010 – new regime applies as employer took action on or after 6 April 2009

- employer takes action on 18 March 2009 which continues beyond 5 April 2009. Mrs X submits a written grievance on 16 June 2009. The action underpinning the grievance continues after the grievance was submitted (and the time limit for bringing the claim does not start to run). Mrs X makes an employment tribunal claim on 16 November 2009. The case is heard at an employment tribunal in February 2010 – old regime applies as where an act begins on or before 5 April 2009 and continues, and the grievance is submitted on or before 4 July, the old regime applies.

Employer takes action which forms the basis of a grievance with a 6 month time limit, e.g. an equal pay claim:
- employer takes action on 10 January 2009 which continues beyond 6 April 2009. Mrs I submits a written grievance on 7 April 2009. The case is heard at an employment tribunal in December 2009 – old regime applies as where an act begins before 6 April 2009 and continues, and the grievance is put in (or ET1 presented) on or before 4 October the old regime applies

- employer takes action on 10 January 2009 which continues until 9 January 2010. Miss J submits a written grievance on 10 January 2010 and makes an ET1 claim – new regime applies as although may have had grounds for a grievance before 6 April 2009, the written grievance has been made (or ET1 presented) after 4 October 2009

- employer takes action on 5 April 2009 which continues until 5 May 2009. Mr K submits a written grievance on 5 June 2009, makes an ET1 Claim on 3 October 2009 and the case is heard by an employment tribunal in January 2010 – old regime applies as written grievance submitted (or ET1 presented) before 4 October 2009

- employer takes action on 5 April 2009 which continues until 5 November 2009, Mrs L submits written grievance on 7 November 2009, makes an ET1 claim on 4 May 2010 and the case is heard during June 2010 – new regime applies as although employer took action before 6 April 2009, this action continued beyond 5 April 2009 and the written grievance was submitted (or ET1 presented) after 4 October 2009

- employer takes action on 6 April 2009 which continues until 5 November 2009. Mr M submits a written grievance on 6 November 2009, makes an

ET1 claim on 4 May 2010 and the case is heard during June 2010 – new regime applies as employer took action after 6 April 2009.

These examples are taken from the BERR document, 'Taking a dispute to the Employment Tribunal after 6th April 2009 – Guidance on which legal provisions will apply', which is available on the employment section of the BERR website (http://www.berr.gov.uk).